Against All Odds

A Miracle Journey of Recovery and Success

Joe Tarasuk

"A truly inspiring story of a man overcoming great trials and tribulations to discover a purpose for his life that fulfills the desires of his heart and deeply touches the lives of others. Joe Tarasuk masterfully describes how God freed him from slavery to his vices and disabilities and turned even the worst of realities into a blessed and meaningful life. This astonishing auto-biography is sure to bring to light God's hand in every aspect and event in our lives."

—Timothy Sweeney
USN, AD3

"My favorite chapter in Joe Tarasuk's uplifting life story is the one entitled, 'Redemption.' That one word encapsulates Joe's remarkable transformation after his prison experience. When Joe went to prison, he wasn't even looking for God to intervene, but God refused to give up on him! This book is a testament to the reality that all men and women are created in the image of God, and no one can fall so far that God can't pick him up and restore him to his created purpose. Romans 8:28 says that 'in all things God works for the good of those who love him, who have been called according to his purpose.' Joe's story proves yet again how unfailingly true that verse is. In his younger days Joe experienced many things he might have never though God could use, but now Joe has been redeemed and is active in bring redemption to others who need it desperately!"

—Jim Liske
CEO, Prison Fellowship Ministries

"God has put a fire in Joe's heart for people like him. Those who have made mistakes. Those who have turned to other things rather than to God...I have thanked God for Joe many times. For what he has brought to the Camden County are alone. However, it extends much further than there. I see the same passion found in the apostle Paul after his Damascus road experience as I do in Joe Tarasuk. However, Joe's Damascus road experience was a stretch of I-95 in Camden County. May his zeal, his passion and vision never fade as he serves Him who has set him free."

—Timothy M. Rice
Pastor, Bethlehem Baptist Church

Against All Odds

A Miracle Journey of Recovery and Success

Joe Tarasuk

First Edition

Together Bound

Publishing Company
Vadnais Heights, MN

Against All Odds
A Miracle Journey of Recovery and Success

Published by Together Bound Publishing Company
Proceeds from the publishing of this book support the author's non-profit organization, Crossroads Freedom Center
www.togetherboundpublishing.com

ISBN 978-0-9891735-0-6
Library of Congress Control Number: 2013937052

Printed in the United States of America

Edited by
Jan Truhler
jantruhler@togetherboundpublishing.com

Cover design by
Cyndie Widmer
eclipsedesigngroup.com

Some names have been changed to protect specific identities.

Quantity discounts are available on bulk purchases of this book for educational training purposes, fund-raising, or gift giving. For more information, contact us at the address below. Special books, booklets, or book excerpts can also be created to fit your specific needs. For more information, contact Marketing Department, Together Bound Publishing Company, 311 Woodridge Drive, Vadnais Heights, MN 55127

Dedicated to Chuck Colson
Founder Prison Fellowship Ministry

I met Mr. Colson in 2004 at the signing of a new law protecting inmates from sexual assault. That meeting seemed like a divine appointment. It gave me the confidence and inspiration I needed to start my own journey—finding a way to help change the world for men and women suffering from life's hurts. After I met Mr. Colson in Washington, D.C., he listened to me and put my story in *Inside Journal*, the newsletter of Prison Fellowship distributed in jails and prisons across the United States.

Eight years later, I had finished a first draft of this book, had started CrossRoads Freedom Center, and was reaching out to Prison Fellowship for support. I was invited to attend a Prison Fellowship conference in 2012 and be re-introduced to Mr. Colson by my Bishop, Bishop Harry Jackson of Hope Christian Church. I could not wait to share with him how his small act of kindness had affected me so many years ago. It was at this conference that, as I watched in the crowd, Mr. Colson fell from the podium from what seemed to be a stroke. Along with many others, my heart and prayers went out to the Colson family when he went home to be with the Lord not long afterwards.

Even though I did not get to meet with Mr. Colson, Prison Fellowship continues to influence my life. It was three graduates from their Centurion's Program that have developed into core members of the team supporting Maria and me as we develop CrossRoads Freedom Center.

I will never forget Mr. Colson's sincerity as he spoke with me so many years ago. His eyes shone with compassion and acceptance as he listened to my story. His life is a testament to what can happen when a person like me is given a second chance. He was willing to reach back and help others. He believed that you *can* change the world, one person at a time. I will never forget him nor what he did for me.

I am the Lord, I have called you in righteousness, I have taken you by the hand and kept you; I have given you as a covenant to the people, a light to the nations, to open the eyes that are blind, to bring out the prisoners from the dungeon, from the prisons those who sit in darkness.

Isaiah 42:6-7

Table of Contents

Acknowledgements

I am blessed to have so many friends and business associates who have helped me in my journey. I know I could not possibly list them all. However there are a few people that I must acknowledge for their support, including the many spiritual mentors and pastors who have helped me grow in the Lord. I love you all!

Maria Tarasuk, my wife. My father in heaven answered my prayers. Only He could have put this special lady in my life. My best friend, my lover, we are on this journey together.

Bill Smith, the sheriff in Woodbine, Georgia. You saw something in me and gave me a second chance.

Bishop Harry Jackson. The Holy Spirit directed me to Hope Christian Church, it was a divine appointment. His teachings are what I needed, preparing me for this mission. Yes, I am a warrior- thanks Bishop!

My family. The Tarasuks and Owens, who have supported me and loved me through this whole journey.

My new family, the Trementozzi's- thanks for accepting me with open arms.

The Craftmasters Team. What a journey it's been! Thanks for hanging in there with me through all the ups and downs.

All the people who helped work on completing this book. Mike and Jasmin Morrell, you got this project started many years ago. Jan Truhler and Jan Sherman- thank you for all your editing advice. Matt Sweeney- you helped get us over the hump as we finalized the book. Thank you for your constant encouragement, patience, and talent! May God bless you on your journey!

To all my spiritual mentors, thank you for leading and guiding me in my walk with the Lord: Craig Brown and Mary Kay Issacs, Pastor Dale O'Shields, Reverend Judy Talbert, Jan Thomas, Pastor Tim Rice, Reverend Washington, Pastor Joey Vasquez and Missy Vasquez, Pastor Clem

Walshauser, Pastor Ken and Mary Newberger, Pastor Brian McLaren, and Dr. White.

Most of all, thanks to our best friend, Jesus Christ.

And thanks to all – God bless you.

Foreword

Bishop Harry Jackson

King David had a warrior's heart that enabled him to pursue God's calling on his life with relentless hunger. Joe Tarasuk has a heart like that. He knows what it means to pursue God with passion. Once he grabbed a hold of the truth that God could use him, he never looked back. Many Christians today have superior head knowledge about the things of God, but they lack passion; and knowledge is a poor substitute for divine encounter. It is only through encounters with the living God that we are able to keep alive the passion of holy pursuit for more of Him. We are called as a church to be change agents in our society. Whether we are teachers, preachers, artists, athletes, engineers, or entrepreneurs our mission is the same; we are to be living examples of the extravagance of God's love and mercy.

The church has spent too many years constructing its theological arguments and positions in order to make fine line distinctions among members of the Body of Christ. Paul plainly tells us that what matters to God is faith expressing itself through love. Theology has its place, but if it's not co-anchored in lived experience, it's empty of power. Paul assures us that we preach a gospel of power, not of human wisdom (I Cor 1:17). It's a power that can take a street wise, dyslexic, uneducated drug dealer and turn him into a warrior fighting to save the lives of the lost. Living a life of power, however, takes risk. And risk is not well tolerated by most. The risk is in being willing to start on a path without knowing the way or even the end. It means trusting that God will lead by his Spirit, and not your own capacities. If we are to be a Church that changes the world, that matters, then we have to be willing to take risks and live with passion for the things of God.

Joe Tarasuk had many opportunities when he could have chosen to accept the status quo. He could have returned to his life as a drug dealer. He could have taken the safe route of working for others. He could have let the pain of his wife's addiction cause the end his marriage. He could have settled into a comfortable life, enjoying retirement and the fruits of a successful business. But it was passion that fueled Joe's life. He knew what it meant to be saved and set free. He had his divine encounter and would never settle for less than relentless pursuit of God. We need more passion in our faith if we are to be used by God. The church of Ephesus was chastised for losing their first love. How many of us fit that description? Not everyone is called to build recovery centers but everyone is called to love God with all of our hearts, souls, and minds. That means passion. That means our lives for His pleasure. Warriors serving the King.

Bishop Harry Jackson

Introduction

An Incredible Journey

When I look back over the story of my life, I realize that the Lord has led me on an incredible journey. I was living in the deepest darkness, deceived by the "high life" I thought I'd achieved. I'd started small by growing and selling pot in my backyard and built all the way up to smuggling cocaine straight from Bolivian fields and selling it in the United States. I hung out with some of the people who held the keys to the city of Washington DC—from bookies and mobsters, to beautiful women and professional athletes. I turned a small garage into a state-of-the art recording studio and became a music producer. Money, power, prestige, and the best cocaine in town, they were all mine. I was on a mission to see how far I could go living life in the fast lane. That mission almost destroyed me.

I've seen the inside of a mental hospital not once, but twice. I've also stared at the unforgiving gray walls of a jail cell. Neither are pretty places. Neither are places you ever want to spend the night in, let alone have an extended stay. I crashed my car and almost killed myself in the process. I was sucked into the hypnotic allure of a cult of musicians who wanted to revolutionize the world through their music. The FBI and DEA tailed me, while the dark spirits of deceit, shame, and addiction haunted me.

The "high life" didn't live up to its promises. The glamour and excitement quickly wore off. I needed more and more thrills to satisfy the thirst in my soul, to hide the deep sense of shame I felt.

Only Jesus Christ could have brought me to where I am now; only the Lord could've brought me from bondage to freedom, from death to life. God's provision and grace have seen me through the dark moments—moments when I thought the darkness would consume me. The Holy Spirit was with me even when I didn't know it was His hand that was guiding me, and He's never stopped sending me signs, lighting my way toward Him.

Chapter 1

Roots Run Deep

When I was very young, maybe around five, I over-heard my mother having a conversation with a friend. "Joey was the mistake in the family," she confessed. She only let this admission slip once, but it was something that flew by in a moment but stayed with me forever. My parents weren't expecting me to be born. Adding another mouth to feed amongst the two they already had, was a troublesome financial burden. Money had always been a problem for them since they married. Like their families before them, money was the cause of much heartache.

My dad's parents emigrated from Russia in 1914. Like most immigrants at the time, they entered the United States through Ellis Island, hoping for a new life in the land of opportunity. In Russia, my grandfather had been a Cossack in the Russian army. Cossacks were a glorified branch of the Russian cavalry service, and my grandfather must have inherited a proud heritage from them. So I can imagine that once they were in the United States, poor and isolated by the language barrier (neither my grandfather or grandmother spoke much English), living in a shack with no running water, an outhouse, and pot-bellied stove must have been an overwhelming difficulty. My paternal grand-parents had a very turbulent relationship. My grandfather, often frustrated by unemployment, frequently let his anger turn into violence against my grandmother. Stripped of everything he knew, he gave in to feelings of emasculation and impotence. He joined the ranks of men who abandon their families when they don't know what else to do. When my dad was 15, my grandfather left his family and returned to Russia, his homeland. That is where he died.

As the eldest son, Frank Tarasuk, my father, now carried the responsibility to support the family. With his mother and three younger brothers counting on him, Dad decided to join the Navy in 1932— he was sixteen. His younger brothers followed in his footsteps. Dad, a career military man, stayed in the Navy for 35 years. Once he got out, he found it hard to adjust to civilian life. For most of my life there was a gulf between Dad and me, distance that I didn't understand while I was growing up. I see now that he would've had to overcome almost insurmountable odds to be the warm, affectionate father I craved. He had had no example set for him.

My parents couldn't have been more opposite. Just as Dad grew up poor, my mother, Patricia Mahr, came from wealth. She was a young, upper-class, debutante when they met. Her father, Joseph Mahr, gained his wealth by being a big-time bootlegger, running liquor from Canada. After he was in a big shoot-out with the law, he quit bootlegging, settled down to marry my grandmother. He opened a legitimate business, Joseph P. Mahr Construction Company, that built Rock Creek Park, one of the first federal parks in the U.S., and many other roads leading out of D.C. Growing up, Mom lived on 16th Street NW in Washington, D.C. in a large colonial-style home amidst D.C.'s high society, politicians, gamblers, and bootleggers. Joseph Mahr was a very influential man around town, and hosted many parties with lots of drinking. He was Catholic, a church-going man, but a wild one--an Irish brawler. By the age of thirty, my grandfather was a millionaire, but he began to suffer from terrible headaches, most likely a result of being hit in the head during a fist fight. He died when he was thirty-three, leaving behind his wife and three daughters as one of the richest families in Washington, D.C. My mother was so proud of her dad, that when I was born, she gave me his name, Joseph.

Mom met Dad in Virginia Beach where he was stationed and working part-time as a life-guard. They married in 1944—he, the dashing Navy deep-sea diver, she, the beautiful and wealthy debutante. Mom lived in D.C. with her mother while Dad was away at sea. They had a daughter, Pam, and then five years later, another daughter, Penny. And then I came along, five years after that. The baby. The "Mistake."

We lived with my grandmother in her house on 17th and Upsher Street until I was three. I was terrified of my grandmother. I broke something once, and I can remember being so frightened that she would find out that I ran upstairs and hid from her. The air felt thick with darkness, and as a child I think I was especially sensitive to it. My grandmother was an alcoholic. She eventually passed that legacy on to my mother, who became an alcoholic by the time she was thirty-five.

My grandfather's house.
He died a millionaire at 33.

If it weren't for our maid, an African American woman named Rose Lee, I don't know who I would've gone to when I was afraid. Rose Lee was warm, maternal, and loving. I felt safe with her and special. The safety she imparted to me would stay with me for the rest of my life and become an important part of my spiritual growth.

In 1956, we moved out of my grandmother's house and away from D.C. to a small, two bedroom house on four acres in Silver Spring, Maryland. We lived about a half-mile down the end of an old, dirt road. I slept in a crib in my parents' room until I was about six or seven. Penny had her own room, and Pam slept on the couch in the living room. In such tight quarters, and living on Dad's paltry Navy income, it was almost impossible for fights not to happen. My parents tried to make it, but Mom was pushing it financially, and it never seemed to happen. With her background, material wealth had always been important to her. As my parents argued more and more, my mother drank more and more. Dad drank some too, and even at five years old, I noticed that it changed their personalities, and I couldn't understand it. There was no affection or hugs and kisses at all in our family. I never saw my parents display affection toward each other. My earliest memories of my mom are of her complaints and her tears.

So, as a child I took refuge in the outdoors. I would build forts in the woods imitating Johnny Weissmuller, Tarzan, my T.V. hero. I just loved the freedom that being outside could bring. It was a relief to escape all the tension and negativity that I absorbed in the house. Outside, I didn't have to worry about hearing harsh, raised voices speaking angry words. Even so, I longed to have a relationship with Dad, but he simply just wasn't around enough, and when he was, he had no idea how to communicate with me. He did teach me how to shoot a shotgun, took me fishing and played catch with me once or twice. I remember running inside the house to try and get Dad to play with me, but he would be reading the paper, locked in his own world. He wasn't always unavailable. He could be supportive in impersonal ways—if I wanted something material, he would chip in. When I wanted a go-cart, he encouraged me to save for it, and then he paid half. To earn money I had a paper route and I cut grass. I was blessed with a mechanical mind. I liked riding my mini-bike or tinkering with old cars. Dad would engage me on that level, but never deeper. He wasn't around much since he taught Navy reserve training. So when he was at home, I wanted to be with him as much as I could. Though he never completely abandoned us as his father had before him, emotionally he was as guarded as one of the ships he served on in the Navy. The distance hurt me deeply.

There was no one in my family that I was particularly close to except one of my dad's brothers, Uncle John. "Wild Uncle Johnny" was my hero and the only role model I had. He was a handsome and funny man's man; everything I wanted to be. He'd been in the Army. He had a tattoo on his arm. He lifted weights. And, he always seemed to be driving a new Cadillac, usually black and convertible. When he hung out with me, Uncle John had the best stories, and he even let me help him tune up his Caddies, giving me sneak peeks at the magazines of scantily-clad women strewn throughout the car. He drank with my parents. But, it didn't matter, because I was always excited to see him. He filled my head with stories about meeting great athletes and movie stars in his bar in Florida and even one about smuggling guns into South America. I was in seventh heaven. When he eventually got arrested, I begged Mom and Dad to bail him out, which they finally did.

At this time in my life, my oldest sister, Pam, was more like a mother to me. Her fiancé, Walter, didn't drink and was willing to spend time with me. He was a man I could look up to. The three of us took trips to the mountains, went to a country music festival, and did any number of cultural activities. About once a month in the summer, we would go to Ocean City for a day at the beach together. I enjoyed the time I spent with them. It was a break from the pain of my dysfunctional home life. When Pam and Walter got married, he joined the Air Force and was stationed in England. They moved, and there was a three year gap in my relationship with my sister.

Though I loved my sister and Uncle Johnny, neither one could fill the void of having a real father figure. I needed my earthly father, and even more so, I needed to know my heavenly Father. Our family wasn't very religious. We only went to Catholic Mass on Christmas and Easter, so I had no real concept of who God was or who the Lord could be to me. Despite my lack of understanding, I grew up sensing there was something out there. One time I even tried to confess my sins to a priest, but since I hadn't been confirmed as a Catholic, he couldn't speak with me. I didn't understand why this man wouldn't speak to me. I was trying to reach out to God, I just didn't know how. Later as I looked back on my life and I could see how God reached out to me many times.

I was about six years old when I had my first experience of the spiritual world. It wasn't much, but it was the beginning of opening my mind to a reality beyond what we see and feel. It was a beautiful, sunny day, the kind of day you live for as a kid. I had gone outside to take out the trash. As my eyes scanned our house and I glanced up at a nearby pine tree, I thought I saw something there against the blue backdrop of sky—a figure, human, but not at all human, wispy and floating; more than a cloud, it looked like an angel! Mom always talked to us a lot about guardian angels, and so I figured this one must be mine. Peace washed over me, and I stared at that figure as hard as I could before I ran inside to find Mom.

"Mom, I saw an angel! There's an angel outside over the tree!" I told her excitedly, pulling at her hand to get her to follow me quickly. When she came outside to look, there was nothing there.

"It was right there!" I pointed to the top of the pine tree, trying to keep the disappointment out of my voice.

Mom just smiled a little, shrugged her shoulders, and went back inside.

Later that night, as I tried to explain to the rest of the family what I saw, I went to *The Book of Knowledge*, an encyclopedia set that we owned. In it, I found a colorful picture of a beautiful angel, wispy and ethereal, just like the figure I'd seen earlier in the tree. I showed them the picture, but as often happens, when children try to con-vince adults they've had a fantastic experience—no one took me very seriously. Now, I don't know if what I saw was really an angel or just a cloud, but whatever it was, it gave me a sense of peace that I hadn't felt before that. It made me start believing that *Someone* was watching over me and keeping me safe.

This belief though would be abruptly shattered by what happened the following year. One day during the summer I when I was seven, I was in a nearby barn playing in the hayloft and building a fort with several other kids. My parents had been fighting again, and I was happy to be outside, living in the imagined world of adventure that comes so easily to children. I had no idea that this day would become the worst day of my life---the one that became my darkest, most closely guarded secret. A man came into the barn and sexually abused me and the other kids, leaving me terrified and ashamed. The walk back to the house from the barn took about twenty minutes. I remember my feet being heavy and each step was labored. As I walked up to the house, I saw my mom, dad, and sisters picking honeysuckle, and they seemed so innocent and happy in that moment that it intensified my shame. The man had threatened me and told me not to tell anyone. So, out of fear, I was silent. A darkness was imprinted on my mind and heart that day.

Several years later, a man, who looked like my abuser, came to visit Dad. He seemed to be a recent Navy graduate, as he was in his dress uniform. Being a Navy guy himself, my father quickly welcomed him as if he was an old friend. But as for me, I felt the fear and darkness wash over me once again. I felt betrayed by my dad for befriending this man. In my mind, he was the one who had so damaged me. It further solidified my need to hide what had happened.

Around this time I started having trouble at school. Reading and writing were especially difficult. The letters never seemed to be in the right place, or I could never put them in the right order. I watched my classmates gain their rudimentary mastery over the English language, while I lagged behind, unable to make sense of certain words and sentences. Later, much later, after my time in jail, I discovered that I was dyslexic, a condition my teachers didn't even know existed at the time. I became a master at hiding my difficulties from both teachers and classmates. My self-esteem was low and I felt less and less secure as my isolation grew. No one in my family took any notice of my struggles. They were so caught up in their own turmoil. At eight years old, I was already on my own to try and figure out life.

I had been attending Cloverly Elementary School but never seemed to "get" what my teachers tried to teach me. My reading disability prevented me from advancing academically, and no one knew how to help me. So in 1962 at nine years old, I was placed in Hillcrest, a "special school" in D.C. where I was supposed to learn to read and write. The drive to Hillcrest from our house in Silver Spring was about an hour long drive, and though I carpooled with some other kids, it was still stressful on me and my mom. I'd overheard my parents talking about money and knew that they had to borrow money from my grandmother to send me there. This was my parents' way of trying to help me. They knew I had problems reading, yet neither of them would sit down and help me with homework. There was no communication about it growing up. Hillcrest also told my mom not to encourage me in any religion. They thought it would be too tough for me to be involved in any kind of church setting. Despite this advice, the school did take the students on a field trip to visit several local religious churches, mosques, and synagogues, but no one really talked about what it meant to have a faith or explained what these religions were all about.

Hillcrest harbored many different kinds of kids, from burn victims to kids struggling with ADD. They focused on small classroom sizes—there were around 10-12 kids per class—so that each child might benefit from more attention. Each child also went to therapy once or twice a week. One of the few things I enjoyed there were the guitar lessons I was allowed to take. I played the electric guitar and loved it. The therapy wasn't all bad, since it allowed me to get out of school for a few hours at a time.

My therapist was a nice guy, and we often took walks down the block during our therapy sessions. I liked to do models, and he bought me a model. I liked walking down the D.C. sidewalks, but as my therapist would try and draw me out, and talk to me about my problems, I resisted. I'd forged my own world, a place that was separate from my parents arguing and drinking, separate from the sexual abuse. Those things were so deeply hidden that no one was going to draw the shame out of me. No one talked at home about these things either, so why should I start now?

So, I didn't feel like therapy helped at all. I just went along with the program, but I didn't understand how it was supposed to help me read. I faked being sick a lot, so I could get back to the boys' world of building forts and tree houses in the woods, and swinging from rope swings.

I spent two years at Hillcrest, passing fifth and sixth grade successfully. I was doing better academically, so for seventh grade, it was back to public school.

Not much had changed once I was back in public school. I didn't feel any more academically confident and this was high school, so it was more difficult (back then high school ran from seventh to twelfth grade). I was so ashamed as I tried to keep up with the other kids, but I couldn't. I'd written a short story about my Uncle Johnny's adventures that I was very proud of, but it came back covered in red ink. I would sit in the classroom, staring out the window, waiting for the bell to ring so I could get back outside. I felt very uncomfortable whenever I had to get in front of the class to spell or read something. Soon, they put me in another "special" classroom. It was on the other side of the school, about 100 yards away from the main building. I always tried to hide going there, taking circuitous routes and ducking and dodging my classmates when I could.

My mom must have noticed that I was flagging in school again and came in to talk with one of the teachers who worked with the "slower" kids, Mr. Adams. My seventh grade year was almost over, and she and Dad's arguments had reached epic proportions. Mr. Adams, sensing that I must have needed a get-away, invited me out to a farm for the summer. It was quite remarkable, really—he and three other young teachers rented this old mansion in the country for the summer every year to get away from town for awhile. I wasn't friends with these teachers; I didn't really know them at the time, but Mom said "Yes." I wasn't aware then, but my parents were going through their divorce, and they didn't want me around the house in the midst of all that.

Dr. White, Mr. Adams, Mr. Dobberman, and Mr. Hughes were the men who had decided to share their summer with me, and they were a gift from heaven. They worked at the Rec Center during the summer while they weren't teaching. Two of them had motorcycles. They'd let me ride on the back and go to work with them sometimes. If I didn't go to work, they'd give me a chore to do around the house or in the garden. On those days when they were all working, I felt pretty lonely in that big, quiet house, and I worried about my parents. I knew that my mom and dad weren't getting along, and it was strange and scary to be in this house in the countryside by myself. I would hide behind furniture—still followed by this feeling of shame. But when the teachers were around, it wasn't as bad. They were encouraging people to be with. Dr. White was a special education teacher, and he had a great way of relating to kids. He and I still have a close relationship today and see one another several times a year. I continue to look up to him as a spiritual mentor and friend. Marshall Dobberman was the wrestling coach and a good-hearted, country gentleman. They were *all* good-hearted gentlemen. If we were ever in the car together they would try to help me to read by pointing out signs and asking what they said. One day when I was sick, Mr. Dobberman had his mother come, and I remember her putting a cold cloth on my head to help me feel better. It felt like a special love, the kind that I never had in my own family, but always wanted.

Though they tried, the loneliness was still over-whelming and hard to deal with. Once again, Uncle Johnny came to visit and momentarily dulled the ache that filled my chest. I was thrilled with his visit, but that didn't stop the loneliness once he was gone.

I was there for two months while my parents were negotiating their divorce. By the end of the summer the divorce was official, and I would have to navigate the choppy waters of deciding which parent to stay with.

Mom wanted me with her; she'd moved back in with her mother in Silver Spring, Maryland. She was dating her childhood sweetheart, Buck Donahoe, whom she would eventually marry. Unlike my father's family, the Donahoes were one of the wealthiest families in D.C. They owned several big construction companies. But money wasn't all Buck brought to the relationship; like my mom, he was an alcoholic. They lived with my grandmother for a while and spent their evenings drinking and listening to Red Foxx records. I would go to D.C. for the weekend or overnight occasionally to be with my mom, but I knew this lifestyle wasn't for me. Even so, I was torn. Which parent should I choose?

I decided to stay with Dad so that I could keep attending the same school. Penny had been named Home-coming Queen the previous year there, and I was already garnering some attention by being her little brother. As the school year started, I discovered sports. I tried out and made the wrestling team. It seemed my eighth grade year had the potential of being something better than school had been previously. Things would be different now.

Chapter 2

From Athlete to Dealer

It was just Dad and me, alone in our house since both of my sisters had already moved out. Penny had graduated the previous year and Pam was married. That year, eighth grade, was the beginning of a new time in my life. My parents' divorce was behind me, and I was discovering my talent in sports. The high school coaches began taking notice of me and encouraged my efforts. I even competed in a YMCA wrestling tournament and placed in the finals despite my lack of formal coaching. It seemed as if life suddenly had meaning and purpose for me. I had found something that gave me the attention that I longed for and something that made me feel good about myself. I was hooked.

That summer I got a job working in the sod fields, which was great for getting into better shape. It was grueling work for $2.35 an hour. Working hard, doing my best, and never giving up made me feel proud of myself and proud of earning my own money. When I entered ninth grade, I wasn't old enough to try out for the football team yet, so I signed up to be water boy. I got to know all of the players and even got to play some pick-up games with them. I also began practicing with the junior varsity wrestling team before I was eligible. Marshall Dobberman, the coach, had been one of the teachers I had lived with on the farm the previous summer. We began to develop a friendship, one we still have today. As high school went on and the more successful I became in sports, the more popular I became in school. In classes, I still struggled with reading, but it didn't seem to matter as much as I found another channel for my energies. Sports were quickly giving me confidence, and even if I had to cheat to get by academically, I didn't really mind. I'd finally started having a good time in school.

After that summer, I was fully eligible to play sports. I was successful enough on the junior varsity football team to get promoted and earn a varsity letter. If you played sports in high school, then you know what that varsity letter meant to me—it was a huge honor. After football season, it was on to wrestling. By the end of the wrestling season I beat out a senior to make varsity, and I won most of my matches. After wrestling season, it was on to track and field. I joined the track team and took up pole vaulting, adding my third varsity letter to my repertoire. I was still very quiet and shy, but, boy was I loving the attention, especially from the girls!

With eleventh grade came more success. I'd had my eye on Dad's convertible for a long time; it was a sweet car! He ended up selling it to me, and I couldn't have been more pleased. I became a county champion wrestler, an all-county football player, and I almost set a record in pole vaulting. My teachers loved me and did everything they could to help me pass. My coaches chose me to be captain of the football and wrestling teams. I was willing to do anything they asked. I led the team workouts and was a quick thinker on the field or on the mat. The loneliness of my early childhood seemed to be fading away.

Walter and Pam were back in the States and they came to many of my matches and games. Sometimes my dad would come too. My mom wasn't around much at this point in my life. She and Buck were drinking their days away together.

My senior year was in 1971, and it brought the greatest moment of my high school athletic career. I had lettered in all three sports for three years. I went to county championships in wrestling and track. I had a nice car, my dad's convertible. Girls gave me a lot of attention, and I was dating a cheerleader. My success in sports became my barometer for self-worth. My self-esteem was high. This caused me to play when injured, ignore pain, and push my body beyond what it was capable of.

At the end of the football season, during our last game, I was returning a punt when a tackler's helmet hit my wrist and cracked the bone. Despite the pain I kept playing. After the season ended, my wrist continued to hurt, but wrestling season was just beginning, so I continued to ignore the injury. A few weeks into practicing for the wrestling season, I finally went to have my wrist x-rayed. The doctor took one look and immediately put me in a cast. I was devastated. How could I wrestle if I had a cast on my arm? After two weeks of wearing the cast, I took a pair of pliers and wrenched the cast from my arm. I refused to be bound by the cast, unable to compete. Although my injury hampered my season, I continued to wrestle through the pain. I was determined not let anything keep me from the one thing that gave me hope and joy in my life.

There is a reason marijuana's been dubbed the "gateway drug." Many teenagers who start smoking pot will go on to use harder drugs later in life, and I was no exception. During my senior year toward the end of my track season, a few track buddies of mine introduced me to pot. I started experimenting. I knew my sister Penny smoked pot already. She was a hippie in her college days, and I was attracted to that whole lifestyle. A few of my other buddies, Bill and Chris, and I were beginning to grow our hair long. And, like so many other youth at the time, we felt revolution in the air. I'd begun listening to Jimi Hendrix and getting high. I really identified with Jimi and his music. I sensed that like me, he had been through a lot of pain. Of course, I did the best I could to hide my occasional indulgence in pot from my coaches, who were trying to get me into college by way of athletic scholarship.

At the end of the school year all of my efforts finally seemed worth it. Despite competing with many other amazing athletes, some who went on to professional careers, I was named "Athlete of the Year." It was announced at a whole school assembly to honor that year's seniors. After hiding my *dis*abilities for years from my peers, being recognized publically for my abilities was an amazing feeling. It felt like my insecurities had disappeared, and I loved every second of it. But as my senior year came to a close, so did the acceptance and purpose I gained from sports. I was graduating from school, as well as from the sports teams I loved.

Once the summer rolled around, I began to experiment with LSD in addition to the pot. At that time it seemed like everyone, not just the hippie crowd, was experimenting with drugs. I was caught up in this scene for several months, as I wondered what I would do now that I was out of high school.

It was during this time that I had my second spiritual experience that confirmed for me that there was a God or a presence in this world greater than myself. It was after midnight. I'd been smoking pot, and I was driving home from my girlfriend's house. The song I was listening to by Lonnie Liston Smith spoke of a "shooting star" and as I heard those words, a star shot across the sky in front of me. I was stunned. I became convinced that there was a power that seemed to be traveling with me, or at least watching over me. Like the time when I saw an angel in the pine tree, my mind was being opened to the possibility of a spiritual world beyond what I could see.

As I pondered what I would do in the coming fall, I knew that several of my wrestling buddies were going to Montgomery College, the local community college. The wrestling coach there had promised that I would not have to pay for college, if I wrestled for his team. With few other options in sight, I decided to take his offer and attend Montgomery College. My girlfriend would be nearby, and she offered to help me through my college classes the same way she had through my senior year. I was terrified at the thought of attending classes and hiding the fact that I couldn't read and could barely write. But the promise of being on a sports team again was too alluring, and I decided to give this a chance since it was all I knew.

Wrestling in college was nothing like wrestling in high school. In high school, I cared about my teammates, and we cared about our school. We had school spirit, and we did what we could to help each other. I'd loved my coach and my team, and I wanted to win. When I started smoking pot I lost my edge—the edge you need in college to be successful. I was no longer as aggressive or focused in my training. Sports didn't seem as important to me anymore. It felt more like an individual sport in college. There was rivalry, and it was challenging adjusting to that.

I was also afraid to go to classes again and hated the thought of being called on to answer a question. I did well that year on the wrestling team, winning most of my matches. But, since the sense of teamwork wasn't there, and I wondered where all of it might lead. Once wrestling season was over, I was going to run track, but one of the coaches wanted me to cut my hair. I didn't want to conform, and so I refused. My girlfriend and I were having trouble because I didn't know how to have a healthy relationship. I was just like my dad, unaffectionate and unable to communicate my feelings. She left me. Soon after that, I couldn't deal with college anymore. I was depressed and ashamed to go to class. So, I dropped out. I couldn't take the torment anymore.

I started work as a plumber with my old boss, Chuck Small. He gave me a raise, and I was able to buy a new car. To make even more money, I started growing pot on our property to sell to friends. I planted it in an old garden behind the barn, and Dad didn't mind—he even helped. He saw it as something natural and earthy since he knew the Native Americans had done it. After the pot grew, we'd cut it and hang it upside down in the basement. We had a dirt basement that was perfect for it. The THC would run down the stalk, and we turned out pretty decent batches. Despite my steadily prospering little side business, I still felt lonely and lost.

It was at this time, I went to a party and a friend introduced me to cocaine. I was more of a jock, while he was a partier, but the more we spent time together, the more we liked each other. My first experience with cocaine wasn't really overwhelming. It woke me up a little and my teeth got numb. It also made me feel more confident and that excited me. It took all of my attention away from my problems; in fact it made all my problems seem to disappear. The cocaine lifestyle became more attractive to me than the sports I used to love

A gram of cocaine cost $50 or $60 back then. I had to figure out a way to support my habit, so I decided to start selling some. My business grew from there. I learned about how people cut cocaine down (by mixing any similar looking powder with it) so that you could have more, but I wanted to try and keep my cocaine as pure as possible. High quality cocaine was the ticket to dealing with high-end clients. It would help me establish a reputation that was different than the street corner dealers who didn't respect quality. Living in the "fast lane" was appealing to me.

Sports had been my way to override all my shame and help me have control over my life. After I quit sports, cocaine became my new best friend. It was better at numbing the pain than sports had ever been. All I had to do was sell enough to keep a stash for my growing habit and to make sure I supplied the good stuff to keep my clientele. Just as I had with sports, I threw all my energy into this new life. My insecurities disappeared. All my secrets disappeared. And, just like that, I thought I left them behind.

I quit my plumbing job because I needed more time off for dealing. So I started a new job laying carpet that had more flexible hours and made more money. I began to hang out again with my hippie, drug dealing tenth grade friend,

Dale. I saw him every once in awhile in college, but we began to hang out more and more. He was a good cocaine connection, and little did he know it, but he would introduce me to my new girlfriend.

Our friendship however was interrupted after about a year. Dale's father had a cleaning company who happened to clean one of the local banks, and Dale got the bright idea that he wanted to rob that bank. Using one of his dad's employees, he managed to get in, but he was caught and charged with bank robbery. After hiding out for a few months, Dale turned himself into the FBI. His girlfriend Elaine became my girlfriend while he was in prison.

Elaine came from a mob family. She was wild, and her family was even wilder. Elaine's mom ran a head shop, a place where drug paraphernalia is sold, and was a bit of a gangster. Elaine's dad wasn't around, but her mom's boy-friend was a bookie. Her mother was scary and ruthless, and Elaine's uncle was a bona fide mobster. They liked me a lot. I got along with everybody. I began to sell good pot to the mob, and they liked it; they even gave me an apartment to work from—my first hideaway.

I was also very connected to the black community through friends from sports. They even called me the "blue-eyed soul brother." I had small connections all over town, and I was dealing and getting my street smarts. I was still selling and installing carpet, but also selling pot on the side.

Elaine's mom was into creating a free love, hippie atmosphere, so when I got Elaine pregnant, the news wasn't as devastating as it could have been. Penny sug-gested an abortion to us, and my girlfriend decided to have one. Two years later, this girl broke my heart by leaving me. She started dating another guy, so I started dating someone else too. After I started dating a new girl, Elaine came and robbed my place—she took some clothes, a few guns my Uncle Johnny had given me, and broke some windows in my house. That was young love, wild and furious.

I was getting confident in myself. So confident in fact that when I visited Dale in jail, I was brave enough to smuggle in a gram or two of rock cocaine in the tips of some cigars I'd brought for him. While Dale was still in jail, I looked for another place to find a new cocaine connection. My old track friend, Rob, decided that he would go out to California to see if he could scout out any new prospects. He came back and told me he'd found an excellent source and even brought a sample back for me. It was really good cocaine, and I knew we were in business. We went out to California together, so full of excitement that we drove fifty-three hours straight from coast to coast, high the entire way. I went out to just have a good time and see what Rob was so excited about.

After a few weeks on the West coast, I knew Rob's connection in California could really help me expand my drug business. I brought back a sample of the cocaine and gave it to my mob connections. They were impressed and let me borrow $8,000 for that first run to California to test out this new source that we'd found. This time instead of driving, we bought first class plane tickets to LA, and even took a banjo for hiding the drugs. I thought everything would run smoothly, but it was like a wild goose chase. Our contacts drove us all over California, eventually telling us that we'd get the cocaine from someone in San Francisco. I didn't realize it, but they were scamming us.

Rob and I gave them the money, booked our plane reservations and got a hotel room. The next morning, our connection came into the hotel room right before we were about to leave, helped us pack and hide the cocaine, and got us on the plane. When we got back to D.C. and smoked some of the cocaine we realized they'd pulled a switch on us. The stuff they gave us was low grade and wouldn't sell well at all. It certainly wasn't worth $8,000.

Rob and I on our flight to California

I was scared to death about my mob contact finding out that I'd been burned. However they reassured me they still wanted to do business with me. That is, if I were willing to work off the money I now owed them. It was a hard lesson, but I loved the excitement of trying to pull off a big deal. As I worked off my debt, I began working my way up the chain from petty neighborhood hustler to serious dealer. I started to live for that rush of adrenaline that came along with making a deal.

Meanwhile, Dale was released from prison, so I drove to Morgantown, West Virginia, to pick him up. We dropped some acid, and on the drive back he told me about a new connection he had that could be our ticket to the big time. During his jail time, he'd connected with the son of a New York mob family. Since nothing was happening in the D.C. area for us, we decided to head up to New York. Even though Dale was on parole, we took a train ride to check things out and found that Spanish Harlem was a very different world than the laid back hippies we'd dealt with on the west coast. These guys were serious, no-nonsense, strictly business kind of guys. Dale and I were escorted block to block by Louis, the Boss's son. Their product of choice was heroin, and they all carried guns. There were lookouts posted on each block, and once we got to their building we could see guys in windows watching who went up and down the street. The Boss, who was in charge of the entire district, drove up in a limo. He stepped out, full of confidence and swagger, his white hair belying the sharpness in his eyes. Louis talked to his father, and eventually we were accepted and let into their hideout. They wanted to start a new market in Washington, D.C.

From there, they showed us how they cut their product. We knew nothing about heroin, and I'd never done it before. We tried to snort it like cocaine, and Dale got so high, he almost didn't make it back. Once we reached the train station, Dale was so high he went into the bathroom and stripped off all of his clothes. He kept rubbing his eyes.

"Joey, I'm going blind! I can't see!" Dale started to sound panicky.

The train was roaring into the station, and I could feel fear and adrenaline pumping through my body.

"You go, man!" Dale told me. He didn't want to take any chances that he'd be arrested since he was still on parole.

I took the heroin we'd received as a sample, about two ounces, and hid it in my sock. Taking one last look at him, I left him there, feeling torn. I made it home, and later, once he'd sobered up, Dale made it back too.

I didn't really like heroin much, but this time I knew it was a good connection. We were excited about the possibility of making money. Soon, "money, money, money, money" was our mantra. It wasn't long before Dale and I could afford a nice apartment together. We decked it out with new furniture and a new stereo system. It was the perfect "playboy pad." We both bought new cars. On top of all that, our new girlfriends happened to be sisters, and that added even more excitement to the mix. Carol and Candy came from a wild family and there was always some sort of drama going on.

Around the same time, I helped an old high school wrestling friend start a TV repair business. He took a sample of heroin to a friend, and then told me that his friend really liked the product and wanted to meet in person. What I didn't know was that my "friend" had gotten into trouble with the law for stealing TVs from Sears and then selling them. He made a deal with the cops to try and set me up. I went to meet this guy at the restaurant to make a deal, but sensing that something wasn't right, I got up and left.

The next day, I was at a different friend's house and glancing out the window I noticed a familiar looking car. "That same car was parked at the restaurant last night," I muttered under my breath. My friend told me it was probably an undercover cop. I could feel my heart sink in my chest. Not only was I going to jail, I'd been betrayed by an old high school friend, one of my teammates.

I did the only thing that made sense for me to do at that point. I went to an old neighborhood friend, "Little Walter," who I'd known since I was six years old. He lived on the same street as I did, and he was a wild guy. He was an undercover police officer, but he looked out for me. I told him what was going on with me and asked him what I should do. He talked to some trusted friends at the station and found out that the cops had two controlled buys from me—one had even been at the apartment—but not enough evidence to make an arrest. He coached me on what to say and what not to say. I was brought in and interrogated. They told me that I was going to get a long sentence but that if I turned Dale in it might be less. I refused to betray my friend and since they couldn't pin anything on me, they let me go. I didn't break. I called this incident part of my "street education."

After those two controlled buys, I felt I was learning life the hard way on the streets. I'd avoided the law, and after my first mistake in California, my intuition was getting honed and more refined. Maybe it was because I still had that guardian angel watching over me. But I wanted to play things smart. I knew the law would continue to pursue me if I maintained such a visible profile. I gave up my apartment; Dale and I quit seeing each other as much. I moved back home with Dad, and started a new job as a steam fitter using my plumbing background. I was afraid of going to jail and knew I needed to turn my life around. Out of fear, I stopped doing drugs for a few months, but after awhile, the desire was too strong, and I quickly picked back up where I'd left off.

Five months later I moved again, this time to a farm with some friends from high school. I was closest to Bill and Chris, but three other guys lived there as well. Bill and I had played football together in high school, and I'd known Chris since I was in elementary school. It was a really fun time in my life, living with all those guys. We had huge parties with bands, and of course, a lot of beer. At one particular party, we decided to try and raise some money and charge a fee to get into the party. Though we'd only expected locals to show up, and just planned on a "townie" party, we ended up with about 500 people there. There were thirty-five bushels of crab, twenty-five kegs of beer, lights out in the yard and gazebo, and four different bands came. It was a night to remember. Even though we liked to party, we took great care of that house. We even had a chore chart, and if you didn't do your chores, you got fined twenty bucks.

During this time I hoped to stay out of trouble by no longer selling drugs. But I needed to continue to use cocaine to keep my fears and insecurities away. I lived for that high and found I didn't want to live without it. The only drugs that we did there were mostly recreational— some marijuana and a little cocaine. There was a no-selling-drugs policy on the farm. It was one of the house rules. Bill and I enjoyed working together, and this was the beginning of my fledlging carpet business. We subcontracted from a guy named Burt Deach. We were blue collar workers; none of us had a "real" job, but we were having a great time.

Chapter 3

Cocaine and Springfield

Front Royal, Virginia, was the spot where I was introduced to quality cocaine, exactly the kind I had been seeking. I went to Front Royal because I'd found another big connection smuggling large amounts of marijuana from Mexico. While I was there, it was the first time I would have pure Bolivian cocaine, and the high it produced was nothing short of euphoric. It was the best connection I'd found yet. The cocaine was delivered to the house in Front Royal in a sealed diplomatic pouch, obviously obtained by someone at the Bolivian embassy. And it was in Front Royal that I met Delight, although it would be years before we started dating. She was dating someone, and I was dating Debbie, who was helping me with my drug dealing. I went to Front Royal about every three months, staying for 1-2 days at a time. Each visit to Front Royal was like a small foretaste of the big-time, and I got heavy into cocaine. Just as the big-time had its rewards, it had its downsides as well. I wanted to create a network of connections that was like a family. Sadly, I discovered that one of my Front Royal "friends" who was my main drug connection started sleeping with Debbie, and it broke my heart. I'd thought we were a team. The allure of power that came along with drugs manipulated people and destroyed relationships.

I took off to Ocean City to try to escape the pain, hurt, and betrayal I felt. I finally accepted the fact that Debbie and I were no longer together. We remained friends and would sometimes hang out.

It was one of these times that Debbie came with me to visit my ex-girlfriend, Carol and her boyfriend Herb, the Redskins football player in Wheaton, Maryland. We'd become good friends. Carol, Debbie, and I decided to take a cruise down Georgia Avenue. I was having a good time with them, but my head was wrapped up with ideas of invincibility.

Because I hadn't gotten caught dealing yet despite all the years of close calls, I felt *God* was on my side, protecting me and keeping me safe. My nominal Catholic upbringing gave me an awareness of the spiritual realm—a sense of forces and beings all around me. These forces seemed to influence my thoughts and actions. One night as I was driving home, I thought, "To heck with it all." I drove for about 20 miles, speeding through all the red lights. Nothing happened. There were no cars on the road with me. Nothing. I believed I was living in a higher realm, a spiritual place where I could do anything I wanted.

So as we cruised down Georgia Avenue, still feeling invincible, I decided to test God again. "Joe? What are you doing? Stop!" one of the girls said as I sped up. I saw the cars in the intersection, but didn't care. I drove between two of them, and it seemed as if the space between them enlarged just enough for us to pass through. We scraped the sides of the cars, but we emerged unhurt and quickly went on our way. In my mind, God had saved me, further deepening my belief in supernatural protection and power in my life. I drove off with the sense that God was listening and had not let me down.

We went to Carol's house where they convinced me not to drive anymore that night and that turning myself in would be better than being arrested. I left the house and walked outside to clear my thoughts. I was still convinced I was invincible, and that everything would be OK, I just wasn't sure what to do. I returned to Carol's and after several hours, agreed to turn myself in to the police. They charged me with a hit and run, took my car, and I was released. My sense of divine protection was once again confirmed.

My euphoria over "beating the system" didn't last long. Within a few days loneliness and emptiness consumed me again. Without a car or a license, I was trapped so I moved back in with my dad hoping for some stability. Debbie's betrayal was still a fresh wound the loneliness was palpable. I stuffed my feelings as best as I could. My dad and I rarely talked. Silence filled the air between us, a wall of glass I desperately wanted to shatter, but didn't know how.

In the hallway of our house there was a painting in muted colors of a man and a boy—a father and son, I imagined, fishing from a small boat. The simple ease of that picture filled me with longing. Why couldn't our silences look friendly and comfortable like that? I missed the moments I had spent with Dad when I was a child, and wished we could go back to that time. As I looked at that picture, the longing slowly boiled into a quiet rage. And I ripped the painting from the wall and threw it to the ground.

"Joe?" Dad called from the living room. "What was that?"

I didn't answer; in fact I barely even heard him. I was cursing and kicking the frame with my feet, shattering the noiseless pallor of our home--anything to end it. I think my dad tried to stop me, crying for me as he did. The tears ran down his face. The next thing I remember is the police showing up at our front door, but a feeling of power had overwhelmed me, and I felt no fear. I threw open the door, convinced of God's protection. I confronted them.

"What are you doing here? You have no right to be here." I told them. I was Superman, invincible and strong. I paid no attention to their response. "Please leave." I told them, tightly controlling my rage.

And, amazingly, they did.

But what had given me a moment's reprieve from my sense of powerlessness quickly dissipated, and I fell even deeper into my mind's haze. There was no peace from the torment I felt.

Since I couldn't leave the house, I did the next best thing. I sat in my car, turned up the radio (which somehow still worked) and let the music carry me away. The first thing I heard was a Jimi Hendrix song, and somehow I'd known that would be the song that was on the radio. I listened. It seemed that each song that came on perfectly matched my emotions, perfectly answered me. I was in this spiritual zone, where I felt that I was receiving information from a higher power. But gradually, the outside world managed to creep its way into my subconscious, and I found myself sobbing for hours. When reality threatened to push me out of my mind's womb, I fought it with all my strength. I didn't sleep, I hardly ate, and I wasn't taking any drugs. After two days of this, Dad took action.

My brother in-law and some neighbors came to the house and asked me to go to the hospital, and I accepted with no hesitation. I was afraid of nothing.

Once we got to the hospital, I was seated and began talking to the doctor. When it dawned on me that I wasn't there for my physical health but for my mental health, I grew paranoid and angry. It was like a light bulb went off in my head. I jumped out of my chair, backing away from the doctor's desk.

"Now Joe, you need to calm down," the doctor told me.

Then four big guys came into the room and wrestled me down to the floor. I wasn't so crazy that I would try to take on these four guys.

"If you want to give me a shot, you don't have to hold me down," I yelled, shrugging them off. "I'll let you."

They quickly administered the shot of Thorazine. As the sedative coursed through my veins, I was hastily transferred to Springfield State Mental Hospital in Sykesville by a sheriff. When I was introduced to my doctor, I almost laughed aloud at his name—Dr. Butterball. *Dr. Butterball!* I couldn't believe it. I was so knocked out from the drugs I had taken, that Dr. Butterball was the icing on the cake.

This couldn't be real. It felt like someone was playing a joke on me or that I was in a movie.

As I passed my days in the mental hospital, I discovered that there's a kind of camaraderie amongst the patients—a spiritual connection between everyone. I could understand them. I saw what they saw. Regular, ordinary objects became symbols with great meaning. I felt what they felt. It was like this unseen understanding that all of the inmates had. A bass player from the Grateful Dead was counted among our number. There were people in there that knew my friends. There was an unspoken language that was communicated. Nobody else could understand; Dr. Butterball certainly didn't. It was a bizarre little community. It seemed as if there was a spiritual connection among the patients. This spiritual realm was a strange reality and I couldn't deny that the reality was a dark one.

A mental hospital is truly a strange place of connection and disassociation, all at the same time. I rebelled against the thought that I belonged there. After all, that was *insane.* One day, I bolted to the barred window, whose bolts proved a bit too strong for me. After yanking at the bars, three white-clad workers seemed to materialize out of nowhere. They put their best wrestling moves on me, one of them pushing his arm across my nose while grabbing my throat so I would go limp. They injected me with more Thorazine, stripped me, put a jumpsuit on me, the kind that immobilizes the patient's arms by sleeves that cross across the chest. Then they gave me my own headquarters: a "rubber room," complete with pads.

Thorazine is a very powerful drug. It makes you so numb, you can barely open your eyes. Try and focus on the world around you, and you're lost. It's like being completely taken out of this world and deposited in outer space. You have no control over your body, no sense of time, and no real emotions besides dulled fear. I slumped against the wall and lost consciousness. When I woke up, I saw a window in my room, and I put all my energy into focusing on that outside world, on the birds, on the sunlight, on anything but where I was. After two or three days, I could start to think a little more clearly.

I was in this room for about a week. Over the course of that time, the nurse who brought my food and water was helping bring me back into the world of upright-walkers, where things weren't cartoons or upside down. She reminded me of my old maid, Rose Lee, whose skin was dark and eyes were warm. She would talk with me, her voice like sweet molasses, and I could've wept over this little bit of communication. This act of human kindness made me feel understood, safe, calm, and loved. Little by little, I could feel myself returning to a place where I thought my sanity was within reach. It took me about four days to get my head cleared up enough to remember one phone number. I called "Little Walter," my childhood friend who was the undercover cop who had helped me the first time I was interrogated by the police. I reached out to him, hoping to find some stability in someone who had known me for so long. It was reassuring to talk to him, to connect with someone who cared about me.

I was let back into regular in-patient care, and for that first week I was on "lockdown." They gave me liquid meds in a small cup to make sure that I took them. After the week was over, I was moved to another dorm. Here, the meds they gave me were in pill form, so when I could, I hid the pills under my tongue and spit them out later. I didn't believe in their system, nor did I want to live with the fog of medication clouding my head. I was discouraged about the "help" I was receiving. How could these drugs and the two group sessions of "therapy" I'd received really do anything to change my life?

The mental hospital tried to give us small amenities. They actually had a candy shop. After awhile of good behavior, I got a job running this candy shop for a shift. I made friends with several patients. Today, I'm still in touch with one of the patients I met there, and I've tried to share with him about God's truth and love. But at the time, I was caught up in my own understanding of what I thought the truth was. I felt the old me coming back, the Joe who was in control. Before long I'd convinced them I was okay, and after my four week stay, I was finally released.

Dad picked me up, and I went back with him to live. Even though the doctors had prescribed Thorazine for me, once again, I decided not to take it. I didn't want to live in the mental fog and confusion it created. I began looking for a job because I wanted to change the direction my life was taking. I could build just about anything and I had been a plumber for a while, so I thought that was something I could do. Since I still didn't have my license back Dad drove me down to Baltimore so that I could fill out applications. As I sat down to fill out the first application, I was immediately overwhelmed. Letters on the page might as well been hieroglyphics.

The dyslexia I'd struggled with since I was a child reared its ugly head. I could barely even fill in my own address. As the application went on to ask me about my skills, strengths and weaknesses—I was sunk. These things wouldn't translate from my mind to the page. The shame I felt over my dyslexia was brought on full-force, and I only succeeded in filling in my name and address as best I could before I got up and left. I felt so embarrassed that I couldn't do what "normal" people could and wondered if I would ever fit into the seemingly sane world around me. Determined to do it my way, the alternative was clear: I would return to the drug business and make it better than ever.

During the next five months I tried to get my life back on track. I knew I had tapped into a power that was greater than me and I wanted to learn how to use that power to reach my goal. I still dreamed of setting up the perfect drug connection, selling the best cocaine there was on the market, and running the best team of dealers on the east coast.

I'd started laying carpet again and dealing as well. With money coming in steadily, the next thing I did was buy a car, a nice Lincoln. I started to feel better about myself. I attempted to put the accident and mental hospital behind me; drugs were my way of coping. The difficulty with this was I had to mask how uncomfortable I felt with the darkness I saw in the people who I got the drugs from. These people were powerful, but they were soul-thieves, and I wanted to avoid them at all costs. But my habit was stronger than my instincts, and I easily let it run my life. I didn't realize that in my desire to be independent and "write my own rules," I was becoming a slave to the drug runners and my impulses.

One afternoon I was partying at the house of one of my dealers. I brought another friend of mine who was a militant African American and a dealer for some of the players on the Washington Redskins football team. Everyone was having a good time, but to me it seemed unreal. I knew that these dealers were also ruthless men without any conscience. How could I consider them friends? Didn't anyone else see through this façade? They all thought I was crazy, but to me, they were the ones living in insanity. I had hoped to find friendship, a new family, among the dealers I worked with. Instead of feeling secure, I felt more isolated and alone than ever. Fed up with everything, I abruptly left the party. I got in my car and just began to drive, and drive, and drive.

Finally, exhausted, after about 90 minutes of aimless driving, I went to my friend Jim's house. He was another big time dealer I worked with and had hooked me up with the Front Royal cocaine connection. We rolled some joints, and he picked up his guitar. We didn't do much; I mostly just sat and listened to him play. We watched a little TV, flipping channels. I was mesmerized by the television, so much so that I thought I could receive messages through it; each commercial and show we flipped across seemed to speak directly to me. I felt as though I could predict what was going to come on next. There were a couple of other people hanging out, and I started to feel uncomfortable and alienated. An odd feeling bloomed in my chest, as though something bad was going to happen, and I told Jim I had to go. As I was on my way out the door, I turned to him and said, "You have to go through hell before you get to heaven."

He just shrugged and said, "Goodnight, man."

The cool, night air was refreshing, and a full moon lit the sky. At two in the morning, the streets were quiet and the loneliness I'd been fighting started to creep its way back into my mind. I was driving down a hill into Garret Park when the crucifix I hung from my rearview mirror fell onto the floor. My good luck charm, my protection had fallen, and I had to put it back in its proper place. I reached down to pick it up, and suddenly, there was a loud crashing noise and everything faded to black.

The next thing I knew I was face-down in a creek, coughing up water and gasping for breath. As I lay there gaining consciousness, I couldn't understand what had happened to me, or how I got there. I pushed myself up with my hands and looked up at the full moon, I couldn't distinguish dreams from reality. The moon gave the trees an eerie shadow and distorted everything I saw. I didn't know if I was dreaming or dead; my body seemed drained of feeling, but at the same time, the shock of what had happened shot through me like electricity. I got up, stumbling out of the woods, blood seeping into my clothes from a gash on my chin. I saw a bright, flashing red light and absently thought that someone must've seen my car from the road and called an ambulance. The screech of the siren couldn't wake me from the dream world where I was trapped. Before I knew it, I was in the hospital and a doctor was telling me I needed stitches, that I'd had a concussion. It was as if he was speaking to me from underwater. I still had no idea that I'd even been in an accident. Dad and Pam were there, but I barely registered that. I didn't know

I'd even been injured, and they thought I might've been smoking PCP or something. Even when a nurse found a vial of cocaine in my pocket and they hauled me off to the county jail at Seven Locks, I was still not sure of reality. I found out later that at sixty miles per hour I'd hit a telephone pole, and that I woke up in the creek about 100 yards away from where my car was found.

At Seven Locks, my insanity continued. The face of the guard who took me to my cell seemed to be contorted into a hideous mask, one that mocked me.

"You got the devil in you," I rasped.

He didn't take too kindly to my comment.

He jumped on me, and several guards had to pull him off of me. Finally, he put me in a cell by myself. I felt safe behind those bars, but knew I was engaged in some sort of spiritual fight. I was still hazy from the accident, unsure of what was real and what was not. I stayed up all night, at times finding myself speaking some kind of language, but not one I could understand. It was as if I was under a spell.

The next morning I was brought before a judge. "Please state your name," the judge said. "Joseph Patrick Tarasuk," I replied. "Who is your father?" the judge asked.

"A computer," I replied. At this point I was convinced that my entire world was being programmed and controlled by a great and powerful force. Dad was standing right next to me. He sighed and shook his head. "And can you tell me where you live?" the judge was growing frustrated. "Upstairs," I said. I may have been referencing my sup-posed "true dwelling place" with God almighty, but looking back, it is difficult to say what I meant by this. The judge slammed down his gavel and cried, "contempt of court." And, I was headed back to Springfield State Mental Hospital.

The second time around was much easier. I knew how to behave. I knew how to work the system. After two or three days I was coming to my senses. I was calm and agreeable. They didn't have to put me in the rubber room, and I went directly to outpatient care. They even allowed me visitors this time. Debbie came to see me, smiling and smelling sweet. We snuck off into the woods, and took our time getting "reacquainted" with each other.

My dad and Pam came to visit me as well, but my mother never did. The distance between us was just too great. One woman who did come to see me was the mother of one of my past girlfriends. Her brother was in the mob and had been the one who gave me the apartment to sell pot and cocaine out of a few years earlier. She arrived in a new convertible Cadillac. Getting a visit from someone like her made me feel important and special.

One day some friends came to visit, bringing me a "gift" to use before I went to see the judge again. They slipped me some coke. It seemed odd to me that the drugs the hospital tried to give me and the drugs from my friends were all trying to do the same thing---make me not feel my depression, confusion, and loneliness. Although I avoided the hospital drugs, I eagerly used the cocaine, desperate to regain a sense of power, control, and confidence. Like a trusted friend, it worked. Next time in court, I got a good lawyer and wore a suit. I looked repentant. I apologized. And, just like that, I was back out again.

Chapter 4

Rebuilding: My Way

After everything that had happened in those five months, I stopped to take a good, long inventory of my life so far. Visited the state's mental hospital twice. *Check*. Survived two car accidents. *Check*. Cheated by "friends," chased by cops, and acquainted with the mob. That would be affirmative. How far could this all go before I was imprisoned for years, or worse---dead? I knew I couldn't push myself too far without praying to the spirit that was keeping me alive. I was grateful to the power that protected me. I needed time to get my life back together. I would be smarter this time. And, I really would make an effort to come up with a plan to make my dream come true. My dream was to rise to the top of the cocaine business, while running my outfit like a family that would protect and care for one another. I'd seen the dog-eat-dog world of drug trafficking and I knew that wasn't for me.

It seemed like things were turning around for me, especially when Dad gave me a great price on his half of the family property, including the small house I grew up in and four acres. He moved to the beach, and I had the house all to myself. I knew they wanted me to dig myself out of the hole I'd slipped into and that they would support me however they could. I had to convince everyone that, out-wardly, I was okay.

I had a new girlfriend now, Monica, who was beautiful and understanding. It also didn't hurt that her dad was a builder; he helped me start the business and lent me some money. Business came first, but my habit still hung in as a close second. I liked being high, and I felt very confident about my goals. I wanted to establish a legitimate business to help cover my drug business. I thought this was the smart way to operate and not be noticed. I started to think that maybe everything that had recently happened to me was going to work out to my advantage. Other area drug dealers, intimidated by my status as "crazy," were scared of me. Finally, I was getting respect! It was a great feeling.

A former girlfriend, Carol, introduced me to her boyfriend, a Redskins football player who was involved in the drug scene. She also introduced me to Rowdy, who I later learned had grown up about a block away from where I did in Washington, D.C. His dad and my granddad had been friends in the gangster and bootlegging world at the time. So, I felt a special family connection with him. He was a Don King lookalike, with wild white hair and a big personality. Usually, he wouldn't get out of bed until noon or 1pm because he was a big-time gambler and owned a go-go club on 14th Street downtown. Rowdy always had a crew surrounding him, an entourage of gangsters— clientele he inherited from his dad. The cops and FBI chased him all the time, but he was brilliant and always evaded capture. His wealth allowed him to enjoy all of the usual finer things in life, and he even had four or five racehorses. He was always trying to fix the horse races, and he was eventually caught—but even that didn't slow him down for long.

It seemed all the company I kept had some kind of underworld connection. Carol's new boyfriend, the Redskin's football player, ran with a group of black militant drug dealers that could be ruthless. He was the one who first introduced me to crack cocaine. I dealt it for about two months, but it was too dangerous and my drug business suffered when I used it. It tried to control me, and I wasn't going to let that happen.

Deep inside me, however, there was still a profound sense of shame. It had taken root in my childhood and sprouted into my adult life. I kept dealing because it was what I did best. In high school I'd had sports, but high school was over. Now dealing gave me pride in myself and pushed me to succeed. I started talking to God because the more I dealt without getting caught, the more convinced I was of divine protection. My delusions grew as I started selling even more potent cocaine. Sometimes, I would hold ceremonies where I "gave my rings to the gods." For me, this was a ritual for giving up whatever power I thought I had and surrendering it to the spirit realm. I was caught in a very lonely and desperate place.

I channeled that feeling to excellence. I figured that most of these dealers were pretty slack when it came to quality and customer service. They took no pride in what they were doing; they were disconnected from the spiritual aspect of their work. They were lost in greed and short-sightedness. But I saw how drugs could lead to a higher plane of consciousness, maybe even for the entire human race. I had a vision. Now what I needed was a source who could lead me to the best product on the market. I was on the hunt, so I went to visit my Uncle John. He'd been "Wild Uncle Johnny" to me for as long as I could remember, so if anybody could get me a good connection, it would be him. I knew I could trust him too, which gave me even more confidence.

Uncle Johnny knew the "old-time mob" in the Miami area. The old-time mob is kind of like "old money" in a town. They were established. They only dealt with the best product they could find, and their connections were almost immeasurable. Some of the old-time mob were ex-CIA agents and still held ties to the government. I met Barry through Uncle John after that second time at the mental hospital in 1978. Little did I know that Barry would become the partner who would help make my career. Barry had been working with some former CIA guys who had a DC-10 plane they used for smuggling pot. They eventually got caught, but they paid their way out. Barry was a high profile kind of guy. He had worked with Frank Sinatra, and John was also involved with some of those old-school rat pack guys. Barry and I clicked almost instantaneously. I instinctively knew I could trust him, and I admired his easy-going self-confidence.

Back in Maryland after getting settled into the family house I now owned, my high school friend Bill and I worked together to open a business, Horizon Floors. Mom, eager to help me do something constructive with my life, co-signed for a loan I took out at the bank. The loan helped me build a shop for our new business. I was laying carpet, selling drugs, and getting high. Bill and I worked well together, and we jokingly called our operation, "rugs and drugs." After getting my connections in Miami set up through my uncle, it was time to pick up some product and bring it back to sell. Bill made one run with me to pick up a delivery of cocaine. We put together about $10,000 from the business and hauled on down the road. The meet was planned in a seedy area of Ft. Lauderdale at a little fleabag hotel. When I looked over at Bill's face, I knew what he was thinking. The South American guys that walked into that room made it look like we were dealing with Cartel—Pablo Escobar could've walked in, and he wouldn't have seemed out of place. Bill was nervous, and I didn't blame him, but I had to keep the wheel turning because of my habit. The guys asked for the money, and once they were assured it was all there, we tested the cocaine, snorted it up the nose. It was pretty decent, so we rolled it up in some carpet and left. I was hopeful that this new connection in Miami would be the beginning of my dream coming true.

After getting back from Florida, we sold the entire amount of product, and I was trying to figure out what direction to go in next. Bill decided doing drug runs was too risky for him and he backed away from it, but I was ready to keep going. Should I pursue the Miami connection or continue with the connections I had in Maryland? I went to a friend's house for a party with many of the dealers and suppliers I worked with. As I listened to the people and watched them interact I was disgusted by their attitudes and behaviors. They were rude, cruel, and dishonest. I knew I wanted something different than what this crowd offered in Maryland, and I decided to keep up my connections in Florida. Even though it meant more risk for me, it would give me greater control over my drug business. I was determined to build my business through hard work and high standards. Barry gave me the freedom to run the business so that we didn't get in trouble. He didn't get high, he could blend into the crowds, and you would never know what he was doing. The business was flourishing, but I was still waiting for what could be my "big-time" connection. So far nothing could compare to the intrigue and excitement available to me in *that* world. I just couldn't get rid of the dream of going to the top with a real "family" around me.

After working with Barry for close to a year, building our trust with one another, he introduced me to several members of the Cuban mafia. I connected with one family in particular and soon was buying exclusively from them and selling it in Maryland. I often hung out with them, going on fishing trips, joining them for family dinners. We had a lot of fun together. I also worked with a wild bunch of guys called the "Cocaine Cowboys" in Ft. Lauderdale. I met them through PJ, one of the members of my drug family, and for awhile, things were going well. These guys liked me because I knew how to handle their product and get it on the streets quickly. I thought that maybe I was beginning to play with people who had vision like me. The glamour soon wore off, though. The Cocaine Cowboys were just a higher-up version of the thugs in my hometown, using drugs to control and manipulate. I found the Cubans' machismo attitude toward women disturbing. They must have noticed that I was becoming less and less enthusiastic about dealing with them, because the games they played with me were making it harder to trust them. The Cocaine Cowboys just didn't have what I was looking for. They would cut their cocaine as much as possible, and

I wanted to start an authentic business. I had to keep looking.

Back in Maryland, my friend from childhood and former cop, Little Walter, started selling cocaine for me. He and Dale were supposed to sell a large amount of product up in Maine. They went to Maine, but instead of selling the product, they partied it away and returned with no drugs and no money. I was in Florida with Barry at the time, trying to set up a deal when I found out about this. I was beyond livid. I couldn't make up my mind what to do about it. I wanted to make them pay, and I wanted them to pay dearly. I hated not knowing who to trust and when I could trust them. I was looking for a team that would be loyal and trustworthy. One of the Cocaine Cowboys gave me a machine gun to "take care of business" with Little Walter and Dale, but in the end I didn't follow through with inflicting *that* kind of "retribution." It just wasn't my style. I left the gun with Barry, and he buried it in the ground.

Around this time I went to visit Kevin, my friend who had introduced me to cocaine after high school. I'd, been dealing with him some over the previous few years. When I told him I was looking for higher quality cocaine, he excitedly told me about his brother. Steve's brother had been in the Air Force and done some extensive partying along the way. Some of Kevin's brother's friends were talking about being able to bring drugs into the country from Bolivia. Once Kevin's brother's tour of duty was over, his friends put him in contact with a Bolivian source, a woman named Brenda. Kevin's brother had been trying, but failing, to move as much product as Brenda wanted him to.

Kevin, his brother, and I met and tried some of his product, and I knew right away that it was the top-of-the-line stuff I was looking for. I knew from my experience with Bolivian cocaine in Front Royal that this was the connection I needed to make my dream come true. This Bolivian cocaine was amazing. The high it produced was the most euphoric, blissful high I'd ever had. I told him that if he could get to the source, I could sell the stuff; I knew they must need connections in the States. Kevin's brother had had the connection with Brenda for six months, but he was consistently having trouble moving the product. Maybe they were looking for a trustworthy guy to run things. I could most definitely be that guy. I heard from Kevin that Brenda wasn't pleased with the way his brother did business. Kevin's brother just wasn't in the same league as us. Brenda and Kevin talked on the phone a few times before a deal was made, and they formed a quick bond. As the Bolivians were looking to expand their business, I was ready to step up to the plate. I knew I could sell the cocaine. I had been waiting years to get directly to the source. I was tired of having to work with the Cuban and Colombian middlemen who cut their cocaine and made an inferior product. I finally had a chance to control the market. It turned out that they were looking for me almost as much as I was looking for them.

This was a dangerous time for us. Kevin's partner had just gotten busted for selling the cocaine we had sold him. The police were closely watching us. We knew we had to be careful as we started moving into the Bolivian business. As we were getting ready to go big time, the stakes were definitely getting higher as well.

Faster than I could've hoped, Kevin was sitting in his townhouse when he got the "magical call" from Brenda. She was ready to meet us in person. It was the opportunity of a lifetime. We drove downtown to meet her, excited and a little jittery. We parked in Georgetown, hopped out of the car, and found the alley where the meeting was to take place. The sight that met my eyes was like a scene out of a spy movie: A beautiful woman with a model's body was dressed to the nines and waiting to meet us. Her olive-toned skin and dark wavy hair were beautiful. She was poised, confident, and stunning. I had a moment of panic: *Was she CIA?* When Brenda greeted me warmly in a charming Spanish accent, I was taken aback at how simple it was for me to trust her. For one thing, this intoxicating woman seemed to trust me. We worked out the details: Kevin would be her primary contact, and I would handle distribution. She gave me a package of cocaine and told us she'd call in a week for the money.

My vision was finally materializing right in front of me. I worked as hard as I could to set up my market and get the money before Brenda called again. I did, and it was a success. I had the best product on the market and for the next three years I worked this way: I'd receive an anonymous phone call, meet at a secret rendezvous and make the exchange. One time Kevin and I had a meet in front of the National Airport in Washington, D.C. with Brenda. We were surprised that she would ask to meet in such a public place, but it was like she didn't have an ounce of fear in her. We never knew when she was coming; we couldn't track her. The prices were half of what everybody else would charge, so this was the perfect way to start the market that I was trying to create. The incredible sense of danger was thrilling. It seemed as if we owned the world and nothing could stop us.

Neither of us knew much about Brenda. To me, on the outside she seemed as cool as a cucumber, but Kevin helped keep her calm while they waited for me as I delivered the product. Kevin sometimes worried for me as well with good reason. This was before cell phones, so hours passed while they waited to hear from me.

One night, Dale and I were in a sketchy area in a neighboring county, collecting money that various people owed us. Kevin and Brenda were waiting for us to deliver the money to them so Brenda could head back to Miami. That night I had to keep Kevin and Brenda waiting for a long time as Dale and I collected the money we were owed. Knowing that they would be worried, I sent Dale to meet up with Kevin and Brenda to give them a message.

"We're still working on things, we got slowed up, but we're still putting all the money together so this can go down. So hang in there, everything's cool," Dale told them through the car window.

Both Brenda and Kevin breathed a sigh of relief. Later we found out that we had come close to being robbed and even killed over the money we had collected. One of the people Dale had gone to see was Nygee, a Muslim friend of ours. As Dale left Nygee's hideout after collecting the money, he noticed another person quickly entering the building. We later learned that Nygee had been tied up and shot in the back of the head, execution style, by a man who had come to rob him. Nygee had always greeted me with the Muslim phrase, "assalamu alaikum," which means peace be upon you. That night it seemed as if God was with him because although shot in the head, the bullet passed clear through, exiting through his cheek. Nygee survived the shooting, but was arrested by police after being released from the hospital. Nygee naturally thought that we had been a part of the robbery since it happened right after our visit. Later I had a chance to talk and let him know that we had nothing to do with the attack. The experience, however, showed us what sort of danger we were constantly in. There was always the chance of being arrested by the police, of being robbed and even killed.

The situation was complicated even more by the fact that we were dealing with other sources besides the Bolivians. Jimmy, my former Front Royal connection from years earlier was now mainly dealing with upper class clients in Bethesda, Maryland, a wealthy suburb outside of D.C. I knew that Jimmy and his friends were involved in a big drug bust. The authorities tried to make a deal with him by getting him to lead them to other drug connections. When Jimmy asked us to start dealing with some people we had never met, we knew what he was up to. One of our golden rules was "never deal with someone you don't know." Yet, at this point we didn't know how close we were to getting arrested ourselves.

So I went to Little Walter, who still had police connections, to ask for help. He took the cocaine and hid it in his attic. I trusted him because I knew that no one wanted to see us get hurt. They didn't really consider us the "bad guys;" we were just good guys involved in illegal activities. The "bad guys" were the gun wielding, multiple busts, wild and crazy, dangerous guys. Guys that couldn't keep a low profile. Not us. We consulted a lawyer and he told us to leave town for a week. Kevin called Claudia and told her that if she wanted to be with him, she couldn't call her brother. He'd left a prepaid ticket for her at the airport, told her to take a cab to a safe meeting place, and he'd pick her up to bring her there. He picked her up, and everyone (including my girlfriend, Monica) got together. We had to pat Claudia down to make sure she wasn't wired. For several days we stayed in New York—all the while making Claudia more and more anxious and upset. She didn't want to believe what was going on. We had to do it that way to see if her brother had gotten to her.

Once we got back from New York, I knew I had to keep a very low profile. Jimmy put together another deal, and we knew it was hot, so we didn't touch it. Kevin started getting calls from people that he didn't really know asking him to do deals with them. There was another huge tipoff that the deals were hot. These were people associated with his work place, people that he'd met during his day job installing fire and burglar alarms.

The pressure of our dealing was getting to Kevin and it wasn't long before he backed out of our drug team. The tipping point came when he had an accident with a lawn mower and lost one of his thumbs. When this happened I was on a plane, and suddenly I had an enormous pain in *my* thumb. As soon as I got off the plane, I called around to see if my friends were okay. I talked to Kevin's wife and found out what happened. The accident, combined with

Kevin's growing family (he now had several children), were enough to make him start slowing down. He didn't quit using at the time, but our partnership faded.

After about three years, word got out in Bolivia that Barry and I were the ones to deal with in the U.S. Brenda and Kevin were eventually phased out of the picture, as the Big Boss wanted to deal directly with us. Soon we were meeting with the Bolivian family directly. We first met the Big Boss in a hotel in Miami. After that we'd also meet with Bolivian generals who worked for the Big Boss bringing in shipments of cocaine to the U.S.—sometimes in Miami, sometimes in D.C. After the first few meetings, I didn't have to be there anymore. I trusted Barry to take care of everything. The Bolivian mob had a policeman in Miami who would hide things for me and keep it for a while if there was a need.

This was an intense time because I never knew if the next situation could be a setup. I never knew for sure who was really on my side and who might be a plant from the authorities. I dealt with a lot of different people and couldn't afford to let my guard down. Very few people knew where I was or what I was doing. If I had no patterns, it would be harder to trace my activities. I couldn't help but wonder, *was our government* letting *this happen?* One of my dealers was even selling to high ranking government officials in D.C. No matter how long it took or how many dangerous situations I put myself in, it was worth it. I knew it took time to establish myself with this new source, but their stuff was so pure, it seemed well worth it. I had the best in town, and I was finally controlling the market. My cocaine use was a twenty-four hour a day habit. I drank Crown Royal whiskey to keep me calmed down. Despite the out of control drug use, this was my dream. I was going to live my dream for as long as I could.

The Big Boss came up to my house in Maryland with Barry. We partied, drank together, and had a good time. He'd been talking about bringing us into the family, and all of the sudden he was talking about bringing us down to Bolivia. Finally a new day dawned, making the dream even more vivid. My invitation to join the Boss and his family in Bolivia was evidence that they felt I was ready to take dealing to the next level.

It was the early eighties. This trip to Bolivia marked the height of my drug trafficking career. The Boss was flying my new girlfriend Stephanie, Barry, and me down to South America to solidify our partnership. "Gringos" were not often welcomed so warmly into the family, and it was an unbelievable dream come true for me. I was meeting one of the top cocaine producers in South America and I was being welcomed into the type of family business I had always dreamed of.

Chapter 5

A Turning Point: Bolivia

As the plane landed in La Paz, I went to the bathroom to finish my stash of cocaine. I didn't want it to be found on me if we were searched. After returning to my seat I looked out the window, taking in the country's landscape. There wasn't much vegetation, and the land seemed dusty and desolate, but I was feeling pretty good. I had part of my gang with me, and my girl was dressed to kill. Stephanie wore a red silk, Asian-style dress that set off her blond hair and emeralds and diamonds around her neck. Barry, in his Cuban shirt with white pockets on either side, seemed relaxed and confident in the role of international traveler. He would help serve as interpreter since he'd spent years in Colombia and had traveled throughout South America. I was very comfortable with his communication skills and experience. I, myself, was dressed in a tailored silk designer suit and felt like a business man ready to secure the deal of a lifetime. I exuded self-confidence.

Once we got off the plane and into the airport, we had to navigate machine gun toting guards and the lines at customs before we could head to the Boss's home. We were picked up by the Big Boss himself.

"Joe Tarasuk," he exclaimed in a thick Spanish accent as he hugged me. "Welcome! It's good to see you again my friend." We exchanged hugs as if we were family. The Boss was just as I remembered him—a short man, graying around the temples, dark eyes, and a bit of padding around the middle that spoke of his prosperity.

The drive through the city was chaotic, to say the least. Our driver didn't bother to stop at red lights, and none of the other Bolivian drivers seemed to feel the need to stop either. We stopped at several places where the Boss exchanged huge bags of Bolivian money into American money. Finally, we reached the Boss' house in a well-kept neighborhood. The house was surrounded by a ten foot cinderblock wall with a wrought iron gate. We were waved through, and I had to take a moment to breathe. The high I usually managed to maintain was running low since I'd depleted my last stash of cocaine before we landed. There were so many things to look forward to on this trip that I started to get a little antsy. As we entered his lavish home, the Boss introduced us to his wife and family.

He offered us a drink—Crown Royal. He knew it was my favorite. As the whiskey coursed down my throat, I felt myself begin to relax. Glancing around, I noticed a picture of Christ surrounded by three or four candles on a table, and I stared at it for a moment, thinking of how God must be blessing this family. I was so impressed with the way this Bolivian family supported one another and seemed to have divine protection. I still didn't fully understand what it all meant, but it felt as if I was coming home to the family that I was meant to be with. I was ready to trust them with my life as they accepted me as one of their own.

The Boss' wife showed us to the sitting room where we relaxed for a moment. We would be staying in a large hotel

At the Boss's house

in La Paz, but before we went back for the night, we'd all eat dinner together. Dinner in Bolivia is nothing like the anemic affair it is here in the States. The Boss went all out for us. It wasn't just dinner, it was a lavish event. He was clearly excited that we had come. He showed us the house, and several new cars that he'd bought. Soon, his family began trickling in—brothers, sisters, uncles, aunts, and cousin. Everyone got together to eat and they treated us as if they'd known us for years. With a band playing and filling the night air, the party was in full swing. Barry, Stephanie, and I felt right at home.

After that evening, we spent the next several days sight-seeing and getting to know each other. While I was there, I saw Brenda and thanked her for her role in all of this. She had been the one who started me on this amazing journey that landed me here.

One of the highlights of our trip was when the Boss took us into Peru to see the ruins of the great lost city of the Incas, Machu Picchu. One evening while we were in Peru, we had a big dinner party. At one point during the evening, the piano player played Frank Sinata's song, "I Did It My Way." At first I felt a rush of pride as I thought of all I had accomplished doing it "my way." But as the song ended, I was filled with a deep sense of emptiness. I sat on the side,

Inca ruins outside Cuzco

hidden in shadows, watching the others partying. They were either too drunk to care or simply oblivious to me as tears rolled down my face. I realized that I still hadn't found what I was truly looking for.

The Boss concluded our tour of the region, and we returned to Bolivia. We drove around the Bolivian country-side and La Paz, taking in as much as we could. This was the biggest trip of my life and I could hardly believe I was here. Barry and the Big Boss even had a lunch set up with General Noriega of Panama for when we got back to Miami. The Boss wanted us to meet the General. He was one of his drug partners that helped launder the drug money. The Boss was trying to move Barry and me into an even higher level of drug dealing. When the Boss took us to Cochabamba where they grew all the best coca leaves, our time in Bolivia got even better. He had special connections that allowed for the import of the leaves to his farms, but the location of his farms was a well-kept and changing secret; they never stayed on one farm for too long.

The farms were about an hour east out of town. We traveled in a convoy of jeeps through some dense terrain where sometimes there were no roads. The situation was kind of touchy as we got introduced to everyone who worked with the Boss. The only reason why "gringos" ever came to South America was to set up business and they were wary of trusting us. But the Boss trusted us, and it seemed to help everyone else settle down. After all, we were part of the family now.

The first few places we stopped were properties that housed the chemicals they used to process the cocaine. Then we went through three huge farms all separated with a barbed wire fence. Each farm had a house and big barn— the place they used for cooking down the leaves. Eventually we arrived at his farm where the coca leaves were processed and cooked. One house on the farm was full of Samsonite luggage that they used specifically for smuggling by molding the cocaine into the walls of the bags. The Boss showed us how to make a batch of cocaine. After it was made into a paste, before the final wash, I rolled some into a cigarette to see how it would make me feel. Despite my vow to never smoke crack again, I knew this was a once in a lifetime opportunity and would never happen again. The rush I felt didn't disappoint.

It was quite an impressive operation. The Boss was showing us how much he trusted us by letting us see his whole operation. He even let us tape record the process so we could remember it all! The whole situation seemed so unreal. He'd been supplying me with this pure, virtually un-cut cocaine, and it got you high like nothing else. I couldn't wait to get back home and continue controlling the market with this stuff. No more middlemen; I was working with the source. It was a dealer's dream come true.

On the way back into town that night, the Boss asked me to drive, and I willingly hopped in the driver's seat, excited by everything I'd seen. I was driving along, out in the middle of nowhere, when suddenly two guys with machine guns in army trucks appeared. I thought they were waving me through a roadblock, so I drove through. When I finally realized they wanted me to stop, I let the jeep slow to a standstill and tried to stay calm. *What if I just blew it?* I wondered. *What if I just blew everything?* Sweat trickled down my forehead and into my eyes, and I wiped it impatiently away with the back of my hand. The Boss had gotten out of the car to talk to the guards. His manner was so nonchalant and indifferent, that it helped me remember he'd dealt with situations like this all the time. After what seemed like an eternity, the Boss came back to the jeep, and we were allowed to leave. I realized then that he either knew those guards, or they were on his payroll. He gave me a small smile, and I knew I was "in." It was the final promotion. I'd started out in the street world and wound up in the family. I had gotten here through my relentless will not to give up. And, a power I didn't understand, seemed to be looking over me.

Once I got home, I tried to establish a gold-selling business from Bolivia with about six ounces of gold the Boss gave me to cover my tracks, but I knew the FBI, CIA, and DEA were catching up with me. Every three or four months a group I dealt with was getting busted. It seemed like only a matter of time for me. I knew my double life would soon collapse on itself. And I was right. One of my trips back home from Florida after setting up a deal almost ended in catastrophe.

During my flight home from Florida, I thought it odd that the couple that chose to sit near me kept trying to draw me into a conversation about South America. This put me on guard, especially suspecting that I was being monitored by various agencies. After arriving in D.C, I was getting into a cab outside the airport, and I'd already relaxed as I was pulling the door shut. But a woman approached the cab quickly, and showed me her badge. It was DEA. She asked me to step out of the cab while she was pulling me out, and she and a man escorted me into the airport, down a long hallway and down a set of steps. They asked me what I was doing in Florida as we walked. I told her that I was going to visit my uncle who had a drinking problem.

When I got downstairs to a small room they asked me to take off my jacket. They carefully frisked me for ten minutes, but it seemed like an hour. They grabbed my jacket and felt the collar and cuffs to make sure I had no secret compartments there. Lucky for me, I had just purchased a brand new thick pair of socks, and it was in the socks that I had about a gram of cocaine stuffed down the front. As they frisked me, up and down my legs, over the socks, I stood as still as possible. They didn't find anything.

In the past I had often flown with the shipment, but had stopped when the pressure got to be too much. Now I only flew with my personal stash, carefully hidden. As I left the airport I was thankful, knowing that the shipment was coming the next day. The man traveling with the shipment, however, turned out to be an undercover agent and was trying to infiltrate my Bolivian family. Bob G. knew I was flying that day and we suspected he was behind my being stopped. So now my task was to figure out how to trick him into believing I didn't know who he was and still receive the cocaine he was traveling with to Washington. I had to make sure he didn't know his cover was blown, so I could get the cocaine, get rid of it, and give him the slip. I did manage to get the shipment the next day, but a week later, after this ordeal, I found an article in the paper. Bob had been involved in a major bust with a plane coming from Colombia. I *hadn't* been just overly paranoid; it was real.

Bob was on our tail. When I left the airport that day I went to Rowdy's go-go club and called my lawyers. Once again, I'd need their advice on how to stay low and how to keep from being caught. And once again, I felt a strong desire to get out of this kind of life. But, I still had more to go through before I'd be ready to turn my life around.

I kept trying to live the only way I knew how. I worked for a total of about seven years for the Bolivians. The last three of those years I worked in close connection with the Big Boss. Those years were intense as I continued to take risks, knowing that I was being watched by the DEA and one mistake could cost me my freedom.

Gradually the pressure and intensity of my drug dealing and drug use, along with the growing anxiety that I could be busted at any moment, began to wear on me. In 1983, I decided that I'd build a music recording studio to help fund my lifestyle and drug habit. I had already built a garage on my property for the carpet company, so I threw all of my energy into turning the garage into a studio. Working on the studio was like a breath of fresh air because I didn't have to worry about looking over my shoulder for the police, and I could maintain my lifestyle of leisure without dealing with the system. I had to head in a different direction than selling drugs because I knew I would go down if I didn't.

I'd always loved music. Along with drugs, music was an escape. I'd never forgotten my old high school heroes, Jimi Hendrix and Bob Marley. They were big influences on me, and I thought I had a pretty good ear for music. I even had a fantasy of learning to be a great guitar player. While I could play over other people's notes and had taken guitar lessons when I was ten years old, playing just wasn't something I was gifted with. However there were times when I was so out of touch with reality that I thought I could play and wondered if God *was* giving me the gift. For a while, I carried my guitar around with me, and once I played so hard and so long that my fingers bled. I continued to play because my drive was so utterly unrealistic. The fantasy was all a part of the demonic realm that I was in. Eventually, I got through the phase, and accepted that I just didn't have the gift.

My old high school buddy, Wayne, took an interest in my studio venture. He'd always been involved with music. We got along well (never mind the fact that we loved getting high together). Wayne was the perfect friend to help me out. He was recording a song at another, smaller studio, and I went with him and learned everything I could about how a studio worked. Then I visited a few other studios and also got some books to learn about how they were built. After I soaked up as much knowledge as I could, I found a few friends willing to help me, and my music business began to take shape.

One of my friends was my neighbor, Little George. His dad had always looked out for me as I was growing up. So I tried to do the same for him. Little George was wild and liked to party, but he was also a good carpenter. So I enlisted his help building the studio. He and I insulated the walls in order to ensure the purest possible sound. We also had an 8-track tape machine wired into the studio. I acquired additional equipment, installed finished oak floors, a vocals booth, and a sound isolation room. The studio also had its own bathroom, a waiting room, an office, a pool table and a bar. It was a state-of-the-art place for its time, and building it had been a great way for me to redirect my energies. I was proud and excited by the new possibilities that music production might afford me.

As I developed the studio, the familial curse of alcoholism was catching up to me, and my drinking habit began to consume me almost as much as my cocaine habit did. Drinking, especially Crown Royal, became an elixir that helped calm my nerves. My typical drug consumption each day was two or three grams of high quality cocaine. I used it all throughout the day, but I maintained a clear head so I could keep the business going. I was the man in charge, and the big party days were over. I kept my cocaine use relatively private because I didn't want to be caught. So I was very cautious, and I kept the cocaine hidden all over the place. I had a fiberglass hidden compartment in my car. At home, I had safes in the wall and underground, and panels on the interior of the house that would slide down— my stashes were everywhere. I also built a special wall, complete with an inner pulley system, disguised as a stove with a stone top that couldn't be opened unless you knew how. In the studio I had an underground safe built into the floor in the bathroom and the fireplace even had a secret compartment. I made sure I was efficient in hiding my cocaine and money.

On top of the cocaine and liquor, I also probably smoked about half an ounce of pot each day. Because of my past experiences with crack cocaine, I didn't allow it on my property. I knew that it could ruin my new recording business. I kept a supply of cocaine at my dad's place at the beach several hours away. It was there when I needed it, but wasn't so close that I would use it up right away or so close that I might get busted for possession of a large amount. I thought it would last until I was finished with the studio; but thanks to my growing addiction it would only last four or five months and I'd have to buy more.

When I woke up in the morning, the first thing I'd do is a couple lines of coke before I rolled out of bed. Then I might smoke a joint, take a shower, eat—basically I was living the leisurely life of a drug dealer. During the day I might drink less, but by the time 5 o'clock rolled around, I'd start drinking until around 2 am. At the end of any given month, I'd have dozens of bags and boxes of empty Crown Royal bottles. That was my routine as I invested my energies in the recording studio. Since I had pulled back from the drug scene, my life was much more isolated. My circle of friends was much smaller, limited to my girlfriend, Stephanie, and the guys who were helping me with the studio.

The name of our studio was Flamingo Records. We worked with several small bands and even produced a few commercials. One band that we worked with a lot was called Pierce Arrow that played in a lot of clubs in D.C. Flamingo Records became the producer for the band, and we helped them put out a few records.

About every three or four months, several small bands came in to rent the studio for six to eight hours and record their music. I learned a lot—how to mike things, use the equipment, and mix tapes. It was a lot of fun being able to embed myself in the creative process of making music. I worked whatever hours I wanted, and I liked the taste of freedom that the studio was giving me.

Chapter 6

Music Production and the Cult

So just like that, Flamingo Studios was born out of a garage. This entire endeavor was being funded by me and my gang of associates. I was doing anything I could to keep up with my bills. Ironically, I was still dealing, even though I wanted this recording studio so I could *stop dealing*. But I had to keep the money coming in somehow, and I wasn't dealing anywhere near the amount I'd been before.

Right about this time the Big Boss from Bolivia got arrested in New York, and his wife called to tell me to come to New York because she had more product for me if I wanted it. Since I was out of my own stash at my dad's, and also needed more money for the studio, it seemed like the perfect opportunity to fix both of those problems. My girlfriend and I rented a car so that if the police ran my tags, they wouldn't stop me. I was worried again that I was being watched by the law. Nevertheless, on the drive up on the New Jersey Turnpike, the State Patrol stopped me and asked me if I had money on me. I did. I had a lot. So I told them yes, I was going to Atlantic City to gamble. They let me go and once again I felt as if a presence was protecting me. I knew this trip to New York was very risky, but I kept going anyway.

I met the Boss's wife in a parking lot on the eastside of the Bronx. She gave me the package and I immediately snorted a big line of cocaine. I needed the boost to give me the courage to make the drive back to Maryland. I prayed that the same power that had protected me before would protect me again. I was tense and anxious the entire trip home. I knew if I was pulled over, it would be the end to all my dreams. But I made it home safe. Later, I learned that the Boss eventually paid his way out and returned to

Bolivia. Once again I was protected by a power that seemed to be watching over me.

I knew I needed to get out of the drug business, but I couldn't do it quite yet. I still needed the money for the studio. But the signs that it was time to get out were getting clearer. A few weeks after returning from New York, one of our D.C. dealers, "Boofus," was set up and robbed by other dealers. He was a gangster who controlled a lot of territory in the city and had been successful for many years. There was a shoot-out and he was shot in the hip and arrested. He was out in a few days, which made us very suspicious. Dealers that get out that quickly have usually snitched to the police about their supplier. And that supplier was us.

The Bolivian cocaine was high quality, as usual. I quickly sold it, saving another stash for myself to use. But just like last time, I went through it in just a few months. By now I had settled up with the Bolivians. Because of the Boss's legal problems, we knew they wouldn't be sending more product to the States any time soon. At first I was relieved, maybe this would help me back away from the business.

Caught in the cycle of addiction, however, it's not long before my intention to quit was ambushed by the power of the addiction. My habit had me enslaved. It wasn't going to let me go.

So, anxious to get my hands on more cocaine, I had to turn to another source. Fortunately, I still had my Cuban friends and some local drug dealers I knew. While we were in the studio I procured a large quantity of cocaine from the Cubans—about a pound. Money was tight. The bills continued to stack up, and I was supporting everyone involved with building the studio. The Cuban cocaine, however, wasn't high quality and I had trouble selling it. As it lingered in my hands, I used more and more of it myself instead of selling it.

I ended up owing the Cubans about $9000. I had an English car, a TVR, whose engine I'd re-built. It was a beautiful blue sports car that I didn't drive much; I showed it in a few car shows, but otherwise it stayed in the garage. I loved that car, but I loved the dream of my recording studio more. I was willing to give the Cuban mob my $20,000 car for $9000 debt, so that I could keep my dream alive and well. I was so confident that the studio would be a success, and I was sure I'd be able to buy the car back eventually.

A guy I was doing business with worked with Chuck Levin Music Company, whose big client at the time was Stevie Wonder. As they sold me recording equipment, they also gave me tips on how to make the studio nicer. Rick, who worked at Levin's, also had a pretty nice studio where several well-known musicians recorded, and I ended up getting more and more into the production side of the business. We decided to try and put a band together, so Wayne interviewed several different musicians, and our dream of producing a hit record began to form. After about six months, we'd finally pulled in about eight musicians and decided to name the band Pierce Arrow and practiced several nights a week with them. It turned into a full job for me. Wayne, my music business partner and high school buddy, and I even tried to make some commercials for extra money though I had no real background in radio. We put some decent commercials together. We did sound effects, voice-overs, the whole nine yards. We thought the band had a pretty good sound.

The brother of one of the guys had been writing songs for Prince and he came up to work with us. Another well-known producer from D.C. came to help as well. We were given an offer to go on tour and had been working hard on the band's performance so we could finalize the deal. They were a very good band, and I had stars in my eyes. They just weren't hit record quality.

Though Pierce Arrow didn't bring the success I craved, I did learn a lot as we played in different bars and clubs throughout the D.C area. I'd also gained a great friend from the experience. Art, the drummer for Pierce Arrow, had a knack for studio recording, and he didn't mind sharing his knowledge with me. We quickly bonded as we worked together, and I was glad to have Wayne and Art alongside me. The process of creating the studio and beginning to work with bands had taken about two years, and the whole time I was praying for that hit record.

Then I met a musician who seemed to be my ticket for everything I wanted. Doc seemed to step into my life at just the right moment. Doc, who'd already produced three albums, was a seasoned pro with an incredible voice. Wayne happened to be downtown auditioning for Doc's band when he discovered that Doc was looking for a studio to record with. Doc had been blackballed from Warner Brothers and couldn't get a contract with anyone, in part due to his unusual religious sensibilities that I would come to discover later on.

Flamingo Studio is a vivacious new audio/video production facility designed with one goal in mind—the comfortable and accurate transfer of creative ideas into broadcast quality tape. This goal is attained by the knowledgeable use of our state-of-the-art equipment and our attention to detail, even down to our private bar, pool table and video room.

* Convenient to Washington and Baltimore

* Provide you with quality services at reasonable rates

* Privacy, security and comfort without the aggravation of downtown facilities

For more information on how Flamingo Studio might enhance your next project, please call (301) 236-6879.

It seemed to be a match made in heaven. I'd been looking for a chance to record a hit record, and Doc needed a place to record. When Wayne introduced us for the first time, I was immediately struck by his incredible charisma and presence. He was a black man that radiated masculinity and virility, and his confidence in who he was and what he was doing was magnetic. He had a big smile and a pleasant demeanor; he was a lot of fun to be with. In typical rock star style, he usually wore leather pants when performing and off-stage he kept that same image with his long hair pulled back in a bandana. The entourage that followed him around completed the rock star image. *Now if anybody can produce a hit record, he can*, I thought. *We'll wrap this thing up in six months.*

It wasn't long before Doc and his entourage moved into the house I had on my property in order to take full advantage of the studio's resources. Art also moved in since he was always at the studio, working hard alongside us. With about twenty or thirty people making up Doc's "following," I suddenly had a full house! Some even slept in the studio. It didn't seem strange though because I felt like I was becoming part of a family. In such close proximity, it didn't take long for me to notice that Doc was a very spiritual man. His commitment to God intrigued me, even though I didn't understand him yet.

When we began working together, we seemed to have an immediate connection. Doc and I both had the same vision of producing an album that wasn't just a hit record; we wanted an album that would spark a music revolution —incarnating Woodstock and taking the world by storm. We envisioned spreading the message of the gospel with funky, gritty, gospel blues sung by Doc's million-dollar voice. I had a vague understanding of God. I knew there were angels, and I definitely had a sense that something, or someone, was always watching me. I felt I was blessed to live the kind of wild lifestyle I was living. My visions were coming true. But I didn't understand the spiritual realm. I didn't know how to discern God's truth from Satan's deceptions. Spiritual warfare surrounded me each and every day. Satan was luring me into believing that our work was being blessed by God. Doc's nickname was "The Preacher." His Bible was always near, and he preached on the weekends at different churches in town. If I had stepped back and objectively analyzed the situation, I might've thought it was strange that Doc preached on the weekends, but smoked pot and did other drugs during the week. But I was too drawn in by the charisma surrounding him. I felt I was in the upper echelon of believers because I was beginning to understand the way things *really* worked. Our way began to feel right, and the rest of the world was out of sync with the true word of God.

One thing Doc and his crew *didn't* do was drink, and so I quit drinking as well. I wanted to better ease myself into the very business-like atmosphere they could create around them. They were very focused on their music and without the alcohol, the "movement" felt more earthy and natural, and I grew to love it. We used pot and snorted cocaine daily; they were our drugs of choice. Doc justified our usage by saying that God had given us the plants of this world for our enjoyment, and of course, that included our drugs. I was the main guy backing us with money, and it was my recording studio they needed. Needless to say, I felt important and validated. Doc was incredibly convincing. It felt almost impossible to doubt him, even though my spirit was never completely at ease with what I witnessed on my property. Doc was unquestionably the leader of this following and took a fatherly role with all those under his care. He considered three of the women in his group his wives, and had three or four children with each of them. I'd also heard whispers about the way he "disciplined" his wives behind closed doors—just as a father with his children, Doc was the final authority with his wives. As a man, I can see how it must have been a tremendous ego boost for him to have so many wives, and he justified his behavior by appealing to the Old Testament's cultural practices of polygamy. Doc also used Genesis 1:29 to defend his marijuana usage claiming, "God gave us every herb producing seed to use and enjoy!" We also talked a great deal about reincarnation, and I started to believe that I might be a reincarnated Joseph, Prince of Egypt. It was a great feeling of power, being connected to the past. Doc's teachings appealed to me, and I was caught up in that "truth." The promise of power and prestige captivated me. I didn't realize that I had been lured into a cult of sorts.

Looking back, it's still difficult for me to separate the spiritual realms and distinguish where Satan was and where the angels were protecting me during this period of my life. There has always been a spiritual battle raging before me, and I did manage to catch glimpses of it from time to time. There were so many signs, wonders, and miracles happening, and I didn't know how to interpret any of them.

One day, as I was sitting in the studio, Wayne came in and for some reason, handed me a picture of horses.

"Uh...thanks Wayne," I told him tentatively. I'd stayed up all night in the studio working, and the next morning there were six horses in the front yard of my house and nobody knew where they came from or why. In thirty years of living on this property, I'd never seen horses outside my window. They were stunning. It reinforced to me the idea that I was in touch with a great spiritual realm, that my eyes were opened, and I was going deeper than the material realm around me. I still didn't understand this world enough to know where these signs were coming from. I knew there were different forces that seemed to be operating, some for good and some for evil, but I couldn't clearly distinguish between the two.

There was also another instance that occurred while I was driving to D.C. to see Doc. Before I even left my house, I felt a huge spiritual attack, a foreboding that something bad was going to happen. I was on the alert, expecting something to happen. And it did. The Mustang next to me bumped a truck and hit the curb, jumped off the ground, spun 180 degrees, landed on its tires and kept going straight as if nothing had happened. There was a war going on, and I was visibly able to see it. It was like supernatural powers picked this car up, and saved me from the accident. There were many other incidents like that one, and they were continuing to lure me into this sense that I was connected to a spiritual realm. Past encounters with this spiritual realm got me into Springfield Mental Hospital. What was *this* force? Was it good or bad?

With Doc, we felt that we were special, chosen to spread this unbelievable music and change the system as true revolutionaries. We felt this music could walk us right into heaven. Satan was used my ego to fool me. Everyone seemed to buy into everything—polygamy, reincarnation, drug use—100 percent, but I couldn't shake the feeling that something was off. It was a spiritual battle but very physical too. Everything about us—the looks we gave each other, the way we dressed, the way they talked and sang to the audience—it all seemed to be carried on an undercurrent of sexuality just like most of the music. And, it had pulled me in. I was surrounded. I was a part of them, but I was still an outside observer. My battles in Springfield had shown me that the spiritual realm was real, and right now, I didn't know where I was going. My spirit felt pulled in two different directions. Although I didn't know where to turn, I knew I was going to have to make a decision eventually. Would I continue to follow Doc or would I try another way?

It was Halloween, about a year after meeting Doc and we'd all gone to a party, and everyone was dressed up, except for me. After a while, it became harder and harder for me to distinguish between the person and the costume, until I could see demons manifesting in all of the costumed people. It was the longest length of time I'd ever experienced anything like that. Needless to say, it shook me up. I thought I understood the spiritual realm, but this was more direct and real than anything I'd experienced before. I knew that there was something wrong with the kind of spirituality Doc was practicing. It was hard knowing what to believe when he could back up his actions and preaching with the Bible. Granted, he *was* picking and choosing verses, taking them out of context to form his own custom theology, but it was convincing nonetheless. I learned I could use the Bible to back up my actions. I could continue living my life the way I was living it and use the Bible to justify that way of life. This is a dangerous place to be.

As we worked on recording, we were convinced that this album was more than just an album. This was a world movement that we were trying to start, and we believed that we had God's blessing. Doc was definitely gifted with an incredible musical gift. We felt we were going so deep that we were taking the spiritual realm and putting it on plastic, cutting to our souls. Doc's unbelievable knowledge of recording made him an asset at first, but soon I realized we'd be continually frustrated when his perfectionism kept us at a standstill. I've never worked with a person more intensely committed and driven to perfection. We were working on the same songs over, and over, and over again and making no progress. Maybe Doc needed to stay in a world where he was constantly performing for himself, consistently believing he could achieve perfection. But of course I couldn't quit because of his success in the recording studio and other albums. I wanted that hit record as badly as anyone. We'd finished only four songs in two years and I wanted to start working on contacting record companies. My frustration was mounting. Doc was driving us, and for what? Every time I felt it was time to quit on a song, I'd hear Doc's voice. "Again."

I seriously questioned if this was truly God's will for my life. I felt spiritually pummeled. Even Art was under spiritual attack—one night he thought he saw a demonic spirit in the studio. It really scared him and he even began to talk of committing suicide. It seemed as if we had both pushed past a safe zone and were trying to stay afloat in increasingly dangerous spiritual waters.

I couldn't handle it anymore. I always had a feeling that something wasn't right, and knew deep within the depths of my heart that something was very wrong here. I talked out loud to the spirits I felt were around me. I tried to find the truth, but it seemed to elude me. Art and a few others tried to talk to me and help calm me down, but their words felt as empty as my heart. Unbeknownst to me, they even took a couple of rifles and shot guns out of the house because they were worried about what I might do.

One night, after yet another take on an already flawless song, I looked around the studio room and said, "Everybody out," as politely as I could. And I made everyone pack up and leave the house that night. I wasn't angry, only at the end of my rope. I didn't understand what was right and what was wrong, and I needed to figure things out.

Stephanie had already left. She just couldn't take my downward spiral. My need for power scared her. Polygamy scared her. My talking to a voice in my head scared her. Her dad was scared for his daughter. And, as an ex-detective in Montgomery County, he made sure that I had nothing to do with her after that. He called me and told me to stay away from his family. That hurt almost more than her leaving me did. I never would've hurt them, but I was at the end of my rope.

Chapter 7

A Deal with God

So I was alone, and I wanted the truth. I had called the power that seemed to protect me "God" for a long time, but I really didn't know who He was or what He was like. I knew good and evil were fighting a war around me. I was searching for peace and I knew I still hadn't found it. Something inside me knew Doc's way wasn't the answer. I didn't know or understand that a spiritual war must be fought with spiritual weapons, so I sought protection the only way I knew how. I strapped on my Walther PPK (the same model of gun carried by James Bond) under a black velvet jacket. For about three months, I walked around with that Walther PPK strapped on in its holster. I didn't know if someone would try and take me back to Springfield, but I was *not* going to move from my home. My sister Pam and neighbor Richie were praying for me, but I didn't know if they'd try to call the police alongside their prayers.

I might go out once in awhile and see a friend downtown or visit a club, but 99 percent of the time I stayed home, isolated myself, and tried to figure out what was going on with my life. Was I crazy? What was this realm of power that I felt around me? Was this power protecting me or was it out to destroy me? Was life all about drugs? What was this dream I was following?

The one thing I knew for sure was that no one would take me anywhere against my will again. I spent time in the studio, going over and over the work we'd done. I felt like an alien. I didn't know if I belonged on this earth. No one, including myself, could understand this spiritual struggle I'd gone through all these years. I was just lost.

I was out of money, out of friends, out of drugs, and out of hope. I couldn't sleep. I had one credit card left that I used to feed myself. I was at the end of my rope. If anyone called the police, I was determined to go down with gunfire. One night, I almost did.

There were a few people who weren't afraid to visit and check up on me. Dale would come by to make sure I was eating and get me out of the house. There was one particular restaurant that we liked to visit, and one time Dale went into the restaurant without me. One of the waitresses told him that his "cop" friend had already come in that day. They'd assumed I was a cop because they always saw me wearing the gun. Dale helped keep me going. But it was the night a couple of my drug dealing buddies dropped in that I came close to doing something I would've regretted for the rest of my life.

When Rowdy knocked, I was almost comforted by the sight of his large frame filling my doorway. I knew he was there to make sure I was okay, and on some level I appreciated that, but I was beyond recognizing it. We smoked three or four joints while we talked and watched some TV.

"Joey, how about giving me that gun," Rowdy said, gesturing to the Walther PPK.

I shook my head. The gun was like a part of me now.

"What do you need it for?"

What did *I need it for?* I thought to myself. I needed it to keep anyone from taking me back to Springfield. I needed it to protect myself when I was dealing. I needed it to feel safe. "I'm not giving it to you, so you can stop asking," I told Rowdy.

"All right man," Rowdy shook his head. "Have it your way."

He left at around 1 or 2 pm, and I went to lie in bed. As I stared at the ceiling, disorientation began to play with my mind. It felt almost instantaneous—Rowdy had just left, and it seemed like PJ just floated in, appearing in my house out of nowhere.

He pushed his long, stringy, sandy colored hair out of his eyes as he laughed and joked around with me, but I was immediately on edge, suspicious of his every move. *Had PJ planned this? Why did he come so soon after Rowdy left? Is he trying to set me up?* These were some of the thoughts that raced through my mind.

PJ brought some cocaine, and I hadn't had any drugs since I'd asked Doc to leave. We got high, but it didn't affect me the same way, and so I thought it was a trick. I still thought he might've been trying to bust me or set me up. Something didn't feel right; the vibes I felt were demonic.

"PJ, why don't you get out of here?" I asked him.

"Naw, man, we're just getting started," he grinned.

"I'm serious, you need to leave."

There was a question in his eyes, but he just sat there, ignoring me.

"I said get out," I told him.

"What's your problem?"

I jumped out of my chair, grabbed him by the front of the shirt and pushed him toward my door.

"What the—" PJ started, but I pushed him down on the floor and whipped out my gun.

I shoved the gun in his cheek. "You better leave."

PJ wrestled away from me, disbelief marring his face. "You're crazy!"

He ran out and over to the neighbors. I could hear him shouting, "He's crazy!"

I wasn't in touch with reality, and my mind was in a dangerous place. I could have murdered him that night.

Right when I felt that the entire world was out to deceive me, and my drug habit kept pulling me deeper, I received an amazing gift. Less than a week after I pulled the gun on PJ, Delight, a woman I'd met several years earlier in Front Royal, called me. When I picked up the phone to answer her call, her warm, sympathetic voice washed over me, and I knew that I wanted to be comforted by this woman.

I don't know what it was about her, but immediately I knew I could trust her. It'd been a long time since we first met, but we'd shared a connection back then. When I finally saw Delight again, I felt that immediate sense of connection again. She was exactly what I needed to pull me out of the darkness and depression I was drowning in. I'd been pursuing this record deal with all my strength and energy for two years, but there were strings attached. The record deal came with a cult. And I was tired---so tired of searching and doubting myself and everyone around me.

We spent most of the next few months together. During this time I was regaining my footing and rebuilding my strength. But I couldn't let go of the dream of getting that hit record. Because of her background in the entertainment industry, Delight knew how to handle big drug dealers, artists, *and* musicians. She had worked with some big name musicians in California. The way I lived was no surprise to her. We loved the same artists—she had even met Jimi Hendrix. We hit it off perfectly, and with her by my side, I rapidly got my strength back. Delight believed in me and saw things in me that no one else saw. She got me believing that everything would work out again. She recognized my talents and helped give me a renewed sense of confidence. I climbed out of the black hole I'd been stuck in. But, complete healing was still elusive.

About two months into our dating, Delight got a bad infection due to a miscarriage she'd had months previously that hadn't healed fully. She had a very high fever so we rushed to the hospital. The severity of the infection was frightening. About a week after Delight was released from the hospital, she was caught writing prescriptions for pain medication for herself, a habit she had from writing pain prescriptions for her mother for years. We had to a hire a lawyer to get her out of trouble.

After two years of investment in this lifestyle, I started thinking about calling the band back together so that we could finish the album. Satan had me hooked with drugs and money. Now, he also had me hooked with pride and ego. I couldn't walk away from it. The pull was just too strong. Delight didn't understand the depth of my drug dealing, and she didn't know how deeply the cult had influenced me. *I* didn't even understand the influence they still had on me. The idea of multiple wives was still appealing, and I thought that maybe Delight could be one of my wives.

Eventually, the desire was too great, and I called Doc to get the band back together to finish the album. I drove down to his house to pick him up, and we smoked a few joints together. And just like that, the drive was on again to create the perfect album. With Delight by my side, I thought that maybe I could make everything work with him. Doc and I both thought we could captivate the world, and we put a tremendous amount of energy into completing our vision. We truly believed we were doing it for the Lord. Everything had to be perfect, and the work was relentless. We cut a groove so thick and deep, we'd rehearsed our parts thousands of times. We were in the windowless studio for days upon days. I'd go into a recording session for forty to fifty hours; of course with cocaine you can stay up and do that. I'd sleep for maybe a day, and then I'd go back to work another day.

Art, the drummer, got his parents to loan us some money so we could go to New York and visit Atlantic Records. We did our first demo with the four songs that had been finished, and the product turned out great. So we went back and tried to finish an album's worth of work so we could get a deal. Even though we had four songs on discs, we wanted an album and a video. I had been talking with a video producer for months in preparation for making the music video. We worked with several artists to develop the album cover of a panther lying in a tree. The drive to finish wasn't human. We pushed for each cut to make sure all the vocals were perfect. I learned what it takes to make a hit record. We wanted to polish it perfectly and then get the Lord's blessing. Being part of Doc's cult had convinced me that we were working with God.

The band really tried to influence me to keep Delight in line. She was a high-spirited, strong-willed woman, full of energy and life. It was mentioned to me that I might need to start physically disciplining her the same way Doc disciplined his wives. But that didn't sit right with me, and it certainly didn't with her. There was a lot of time and money invested in that record, and I wanted to see some of the rewards for all my hard work. We were almost finished and our dream was soon to be a reality. The band and I truly believed we were going to create a revolution that would show people how life was meant to be lived. But few dreams can survive without support. I was out of money and out of drugs. Almost as if it were an answer to prayer I got a call from Florida. The Bolivians needed somebody to move some product for them. After the Big Boss had gotten arrested in New York, he got back to Bolivia, but couldn't come back to the U.S. This time he'd sent his wife to Florida to arrange the deal.

I got just what I thought I wanted, but in my heart I carried heavy chains. These were my truths: the truth of the way the cocaine made me feel, the sense of accomplishment I had from being successful despite all the odds, the indomitable feeling I received from believing that I was under some sort of spiritual protection, and the satisfaction of building a family and watching my dreams come true. Cocaine was a tool that would help me complete this dream of changing the world. I wasn't a businessman anymore though—I couldn't conduct business as I used to. The idea of power consumed me, and I was more of a rock star. My long hair was pulled back in a pony-tail and my sunglasses were less of an accessory as they were a permanent fixture on my face. Somehow I just *knew* that I was reincarnated; I was Joseph, Prince of Egypt. And I could do anything. I was convinced that Joseph's spirit was mine. I finally really bought into the cult's ideas about reincarnation.

Barry, who usually transported the drugs back to me in Maryland, was tending a farm in the Amazon of Colombia for a wealthy man. So, I had to change the way I usually did business. It'd been two years since I'd really been involved with the Bolivians, and after getting the phone call from them, I wondered if this was all really happening again. Delight and I were running late to the airport, but once we arrived, we breezed right through check-in and security, and walked right on the plane five minutes before departure. We shouldn't have made that flight, but somehow we did. This just added to my feelings of invincibility, that something greater than me was guiding me. On the plane to Florida, I was sane enough to realize that I was in no condition to drive the cocaine from Florida to Maryland, but not sane enough to say no. I was invincible after all.

Although I sensed spiritual guidance on my side, I also thought I saw signs and spirits everywhere. I attached great significance to things I saw, believing there were messages hidden in them for me. I had always paid attention to things around me, and it had kept me from being arrested for a long time. But this trip was not my normal mode of operation and it was putting me at great risk. I was on hyper alert, and it was getting to me. My paranoia was on the verge of overwhelming me. Delight was by my side, but she didn't really know what this trip was about. She caught my hand and squeezed it, and immediately I felt a small oasis of peace in the midst of my own inner turmoil. I knew I needed answers to the questions that had been bombarding my mind for so long. What was reality? Was there more to this life than I knew? What was right? What was wrong? I knew I was at the most significant crossroads of my life. If I returned home I would be right back into the chaos of Doc and his cult; I wouldn't have the strength to resist it any longer. I was desperate to hear from God and find another way. I wanted to make a deal.

Lord, I said inwardly, *if I get caught this time, I give up! I give my life to you.*

It was a relief to breathe these words quietly to Him but also a challenge. I hadn't been caught yet. And if I made this trip, it could be my last. The band was talking about doing a promotion video, we'd just designed the album cover, and I just needed some money to finish the dream.

Delight and I landed in Miami, and I used the license and money that I'd borrowed from a friend to rent a Cadillac. Normally Barry took the pressure off me and took care of things like this so I could be completely aware of my surroundings, but now was different. We were quickly on our way to meet the family at an international hotel right on the ocean that we had met at many times before. I'd met some of the Bolivian army generals there, and I'd also met the Big Boss there in times past. The pressure I'd already been feeling began to escalate. I hadn't been sleeping, and the line between reality and my delusions was dangerously blurred. Barry was the one that kept me from getting into trouble and helped me focus. Without him, I found myself making sloppy and irrational decisions.

Delight and I got settled in our room, and some of my Cuban friends I had in Miami came to visit us in our room. I told them about the record I was producing and played them a tape of some of the songs from our record. I was full of bravado and bragged to them that our record was huge, and we were going to make millions of dollars. They had never seen me act this way before—with my long hair and sunglasses, I was dressed like a rock star, not the businessman they'd come to know, and as I played them the tape, I could see them eye me with curiosity. They knew I'd been working on this for two years. It didn't matter to them how I looked; they still trusted me and knew I'd come through for them. What they didn't under-stand was that in my mind, my new persona was all about finding the truth, and I was on the path to find it.

Later, I went to meet the Bolivians. Inside I was a wreck, but outwardly I kept my cool and convinced them that selling the cocaine was no problem. When I walked into that hotel room, the Bolivians greeted me as they always had--like family. I was loyal to them, and they really were my family. My attitude about business had changed, but my attitude toward them had not.

I didn't get the whole amount of cocaine at that time since they didn't keep it in their room anyway, but I did get a large sample of the product. I took it back my hotel room, and both Delight and I got high. It was some of the best stuff I'd had in years. *"This is what I've been missing."* I thought. *"The pure stuff."* Nothing could compare to this high. On a scale of one to ten, it was definitely a ten, if not higher. I felt so euphoric. Our room had a balcony, and we stepped outside to look out over the bay. The clouds were so amazingly white against the brilliant blue of the sky, and the sun shone warmly down on us.

Later I left the hotel to meet with the Bolivians again to arrange for the pickup of the cocaine I was going to sell. Before I left the room I warned Delight, "Don't touch my stash." I didn't want her getting too high before our trip back, or she would get too crazy. I wasn't going to take any chances, not now.

After meeting with my Bolivian contacts to arrange the pick-up, I headed back to the hotel. When I got back to my room to pick up Delight, as soon as I opened the door I knew by the look on her face what she'd done. She'd opened the cocaine when I asked her not to. "Delight!" I cried. I was suddenly angrier than I'd been in a long time.

I crossed the room in a flash and hit her across the cheek. Her eyes registered incredulity, then pain, and then anger. And Delight, not being the kind of woman that would stand for this behavior from me, hit me back. We raged against each other for about five minutes until we calmed down enough to realize that our control was being held by thin threads stretched to breaking points.

"I'm sorry," I told her, feeling broken by the red mark still on her cheek. She kissed me, and we decided to stay for one more night.

Hitting her is something that I regret to this day. My mom and dad had fought all the time and I swore I would not be like them. I knew that I'd been deeply inculcated with the cult's logic, but I never thought that I would actually reprimand a woman by hitting her. Never in my life had I hit a woman, and I'd hit not just any woman, but the woman I felt the Lord had sent to me as my angel. She'd been there for me in my darkest moments and helped me start to feel some semblance of normal again.

The next day I called one of my friends in the Cuban mob I'd met with the day before. This friend was the one that I'd given my sports car to as payment for my debt. I wanted him to come meet me at the hotel again and share some of this great cocaine I'd gotten. This was the guy who had always seemed to have beautiful women hanging around him, and there was that one in particular that I'd always had my eye on. I casually asked my friend how his old girlfriend was doing, and he told me he'd call her, let her know I was in town and tell her to stop by. (Since I'd been hanging around Doc again, it was easy for me to think—maybe *she* could be one of my wives.) His quick response and eagerness to help arrange our meeting immediately made me start to feel suspicious of him. The more we talked, the more the idea grew that maybe he was a part of some plot to set me up. He *did* have a reason to get back at me. When he came to collect from me in Maryland, I hurt his pride by embarrassing him in front of the girls.

When she did come I almost couldn't believe it. I'd saved some of my stash to let her try, and she was very grateful. Delight and I agreed to meet up with her later.

Delight wasn't sold that this was the right thing, but we didn't talk about what was going on. Delight loved me, and she'd committed to stay with me. I was thinking she might have accepted polygamy since she'd been around Doc and his wives. If we were successful, then that would be the lifestyle we had. I wasn't pushing it, but I was just letting it roll along. I wasn't sure if it was right in my heart, but it was just so attractive, I didn't care.

It was finally time to meet the Bolivians and pick up the stash. I stepped out into the hot, humid Florida morning and sweat began beading on my forehead. I picked up two and a half kilos of cocaine at a remodeled art-deco hotel in an older part of Miami. The beach off the hotel was wide, and it wasn't hard to find my contacts. They took me back to their room, gave me the cocaine, and I was on my way back to my hotel. All of my senses were in over-drive. I couldn't keep my emotions under control. I was exultant; I was paranoid; I was miserable---all at once. I drove quickly back to the hotel, wondering where exactly in the room I'd stash almost two and a half kilos of cocaine.

I lay in bed that night and stared at the ceiling, unable to sleep. *What am I doing? Who have I become?* I was on a mission fueled by an incredible desire to make things work, no matter the cost. Now I wondered, *"Was the cost really worth it?"*

The next morning we were anxious to get out of there. We made our way quickly toward our rented Cadillac, and from across the parking lot I could see that the trunk was open. So somebody was after us after all. I told Delight that someone was after us, and my instincts took over. Well, if I was going down, I would make the biggest scene possible. My mind started racing, and I wanted to throw everything off base.

"This hotel is trying to steal from me!" I shouted. "Somebody was in my trunk!" I acted outraged, waving my arms and threatening to find a manager.

I knew that because of my record, if the DEA, the FBI, or the local cops were looking for me, they would be hesitant to approach me since I was a certified "crazy" person. They wouldn't try and take me while I was making a scene in public since they didn't know what I would do next.

Delight had to practically haul me to the car, and as we jumped in I told her, "If somebody comes after us, I'm going to run this car into the ocean." I wasn't thinking about dying at all, I just knew that the cocaine would dissolve in the water. I would go down if they grabbed me because there was no other way for me to hide it. There was so much energy pulsing through me. I was becoming more and more unraveled.

As we were pulling away, a helicopter flew overhead, and thinking fast, I pulled into an underground parking lot about fifty yards away. I sat there for about ten or fifteen minutes until it seemed that the helicopter had gone past. I jumped onto highway 95, and we were on our way to my Uncle Johnny's in Fort Lauderdale. I knew I needed time to calm down and get my thoughts together. The whole time I kept glancing in the rear view mirror, sure that someone was following me. *Hasn't that black car been behind me the whole time?* I tried to take turns and shake whoever might be following us, but there was no way I could be inconspicuous. I was in a rented Cadillac, and I still had on my rock star hat and sunglasses. We made it to Johnny's, and the relief was palpable. Was God going to let me get away with this?

Chapter 8

Caught! Turning it Over to God

At Johnny's I asked him to close all the blinds and make sure the doors were locked. Even the sight of my favorite uncle didn't help calm me down or make me feel safe. I hadn't even hidden the cocaine yet; it was still in a bag inside the car. I was going to put it in one of the door panels or in the spare tire, but I was too afraid to walk outside, and I knew that I would get busted for sure. My paranoia had grown to epic proportions.

We were at Johnny's for three or four hours, and we couldn't rest. I finally went outside and put the cocaine in one of the panels of the trunk—very well hidden. I kept a few joints rolled up in the dash for the ride. When I walked back into the house, it was like I was plugged into an electric socket, I was so wired.

"Joey, Joey, sit down," Johnny took me by the shoulders and gave me a little shove in the direction of the living room, "sit down on the couch and rest for a while. You have a long drive ahead of you."

And then, he did the best thing he knew to do in order to help me calm down a little and get back on the road. He gave me a Taser gun.

"In case you get caught," he said as he handed me the gun. "This will give you time to get away."

We jumped in the car as soon as it got dark and headed toward Jacksonville. As we drove down the road, I kept getting high so I could stay up. I was a physical wreck. I was an emotional wreck. There was much turmoil in my heart. What a paradoxical feeling, to be so tired that all you want to do is sleep like the dead, but the tiredness is what's keeping you going---keeping you alive.

When we got to Jacksonville, we tried to find a hotel, but we drove around in circles because I thought I'd get busted for sure if we stopped. So we hopped back on the highway, exhausted. I smoked a joint to calm down, and soon we were crossing the Florida-Georgia border, and I smiled a little at the peach on Georgia's welcome sign. It was around 3 a.m. I just couldn't stop. Not now.

I should never have been driving that night. Well, I take that back. Since everything is up to the Lord, He knew that it was my time. Delight was praying out loud for me, asking the Lord to give me strength and peace. Right then, I didn't know how close she was to having her prayers answered.

Through my sunglasses, I saw flashing red lights in my rearview mirror. I pulled onto the shoulder and everything happened in slow motion, like a dream that wasn't really happening to me.

The officer shined his flashlight into our car and asked to see my license. I squinted and shrugged, and he asked permission to look through the car. He immediately went to the trunk and pulled the panels off of the wheel wells, as if he already knew what he would find. I heard him call for another squad car for backup, his voice sounding muffled, like it was coming from underwater.

"I'm going to need some help," he was saying into the radio.

And just like that, it was over.

Relief poured over me. A weight had been lifted from my chest. All of the tension and anxiety from the dealing, the cult, the running from the police and the spiritual warfare, was releasing, like steam out of a pressure cooker. I didn't know what was ahead for me, but I knew I was not going back to the confusion and torment of the past. At that moment I was ready to accept whatever consequences would come, even if it meant spending the rest of my life in jail. Although I was calm, Delight had fight in her eyes. When the backup arrived, they put her in one car and me in another.

Sitting there in the stale-smelling back seat of the cop car, I threw up my hands.

I'm yours Lord. I'm all yours.

And right then, he literally became my Savior. Jesus saved my life. He let me see Satan's playground for what it was: a place where destruction, disillusionment, and death were my companions. Right then and there, he took me to the other side where He gives joy, peace, wonders, and supernatural gifts and best of all, a beautiful walk with Him. He knew he could use me, and I was ready as I sat there and surrendered my life to Him.

After I was arrested, I was taken to Camden County's new jail in Woodbine, Georgia, a town boasting a population of 1,218 souls, right on the Florida-Georgia border. Upon first glance, you might not guess that a town like Woodbine, which proudly hosts homespun activities like Georgia's Official Crawfish Festival, would be a major stop right out of Florida for drug traffickers. But Interstate 95, from Florida to Maine, is the main overland route for trafficking and has been nicknamed by cops as one of the "cocaine corridors" along the East Coast. A watchful eye is usually extended over Woodbine.

Big Charlie, the jail administrator's son, was a tough guy with an arrogant swagger. He brought me in and another officer processed my arrest. My clothes were taken, and I had to change into an orange jumpsuit, and just like that, the only identity I could claim was "inmate."

No real, close-toed shoes, only flip-flops. I was brought back to the cell block where there were four metal tables in a big open area and two levels of cells. There were two men per cell, one toilet made out of aluminum, and one small sink. I tried to take it all in, but the only thing I felt at the moment was cold. It was like I'd stepped into an icebox. I was put in a cell by myself so that I wouldn't mix with the other inmates before meeting with the DEA. The mattress in my cell felt like it was made out of straw—later I found out they're made of a tough plastic so the inmates don't try to tear it up. My one flat pillow and thin sheet were cold comfort on that first night. I made sure to sleep with my head away from the toilet; I would've been about 18 inches away from it otherwise. The top bunk was like a small jailhouse privilege—you have to "earn your stripes" or just wait for your cellmate to leave before you can sleep in the top bunk.

```
                    IN THE SUPERIOR COURT OF CAMDEN COUNTY
                              STATE OF GEORGIA


STATE OF GEORGIA                     )
                                     )
                                     )
            vs.                      )    INDICTMENT NO. _____
                                     )
    JOSEPH TARASUK                   )
         Defendant                   )



                                ORDER


         Defendant's Motion for Bail Without Waiver of Preliminary
    Hearing having regularly come on to be heard, counsel for the
    Defendant and the District Attorney having been present and
    heard, and appearing that it is mete, right and just that the
    Defendant be granted bail,

         IT IS HEREBY ORDERED, ADJUDGED AND DECREED that the Defendant,
    without waiving a preliminary hearing, is hereby granted bail to
    be made with sufficient surety in the amount of Two Hundred Thousand
    DOLLARS ($ 200,000°° ), to assure the Defendant's presence at his
    trial and at such other times as directed by the Court.

         IT IS SO ORDERED, this 18ᵗʰ day of Dec , 19 87.



                                      Judge, Superior Court of
            ROBERT L. SCOGGIN         Camden County, Georgia
               Senior Judge           Brunswick Judicial Circuit
            GEORGIA SUPERIOR COURT
                                         STATE OF GEORGIA
                                      CAMDEN SUPERIOR COURT

                                 Filed Dec. 18, 1987 at 30 A.M.
                                                        P.M.
                                                          Clerk
```

My bail was set at $200,000

As I lay there, alone, staring at the walls, my commitment to a new life following God faced the first of many battles. I began to think of how my arrest was unjust and that I didn't deserve this. I decided to fast in protest of my arrest. I was having second thoughts after my surrender to the Lord. I was still trying to control my destiny. I'd never fasted before, and the Holy Spirit wasn't guiding my decision. Doc had once fasted forty days, and his commitment impressed me, even if his commitment was ultimately to the demonic realm! With Doc's example still imprinted in my mind, as well as memories I had of Christ and his forty day fast, I thought I'd try fasting as well.

Without the Holy Spirit, my attempt to fast was a fleshly decision, and I was failing. Like a dog sniffing around for crumbs under the table, I nosed around for ketchup or jelly packets to save in case I got too hungry and needed to eat them later. That way I would still be able to "save face" and uphold my fast in the eyes of those watching me. I had no idea what fasting really meant and what its purposes were. My fast lasted not even a day, and I was eating jailhouse food.

A few days after I'd been in jail, the DEA pulled me down in one of the interrogation rooms. They wanted me to snitch on my people in Florida by telling them I had car problems and asking them to come and pick me up so that we could set up a bust. I refused; that was the last thing I would've done, no matter how much time they were telling me I would get if I didn't comply.

I was still thinking about the record album and influencing the world through a musical revolution. I tried to convince the DEA that we would be able to work together to tackle the nation's drug problem, but all they were interested in was setting up a bust. When they saw I wasn't going to cooperate, they put me back in my cell.

The battle over my commitment continued as I thought about whether or not to confess. So far I had tried to avoid my consequences by fasting in protest and my grandiose ideas of a music revolution. It was time for me to make a stand and decide if I really was going to turn it all over to the Lord.

Eight days later I asked why they were still holding Delight, and I was told that in order to exonerate her, I needed to confess and take all responsibility for my arrest. The only way to protect Delight was for me to confess. The state was anxious for me to confess. That would make their case against me air tight. There were three or four other couples who'd been arrested for interstate drug transportation, and they were all getting lawyers and trying to figure out who would take the blame for the cocaine in their car. It was unheard of to confess to your crime before you went to court, but I had made my decision. Again, I found myself surrendering to the Lord. I was willing to take the consequences for my actions and proud of myself for not turning in the Bolivians whom I considered my family. If you do the crime, you do the time.

I willingly confessed my guilt, but Delight needed $1,000 for her bail. She contacted her mother and brothers, but no one would return her calls. Her family had cut her off. I called my friend Rowdy and he sent the $1,000 needed to bail Delight out of jail. She was released, which was a huge relief for me. Delight could go home, and I couldn't have been happier. (Unless of course if I'd been going home with her!). The first time I went to church in jail Delight was still being held. We met there, and it was the first time we'd been able to talk since the arrest. After she left, and before my sentencing, there was a three month period of time when I went to church there every Sunday trying to understand this new walk. The Scripture really attracted me; the Lord attracted me. I had been attracted to Doc's cult and his use of the Bible, but this was different. There was no dark spirit behind the real truth of Christ I was hearing. The pastor came and gave a nice jailhouse service, and his daughter came to play the organ. There were about twenty men, mostly black, that came to church.

That third month before my sentencing, I responded to an altar call to come and be baptized. When the pastor announced that there would be separate troughs, one for the black guys and one for the white, I was in complete disbelief. How could anyone who claimed the love of Jesus use race as a way to separate us? That was not the Jesus I was coming to know. So, I led a little rebellion amongst the church's congregants and quit going to church.

My understanding of Christ and Scripture was still very limited, but I had an intense desire to live a life that pleased Him. It was a constant struggle to live against the grain of what was acceptable and even valued in jail. Cursing, lying, manipulation and only looking out for yourself are normal behaviors. Sexual purity is another area that is hard to maintain in jail. Passing around magazines and books is common as inmates seek some sort of escape. I made a decision that I wasn't going to let my flesh rule my spiritual life. So, while I was in jail, I made a commitment to stay sexually pure, and I kept my word.

The day for my sentencing came before I knew it. Delight had to come back for it since she'd been arrested with me. She put a flower and a nice card on the sheriff's desk before I went to the courthouse and tried to open a door for some kind of help with her warmth and charm. She told the sheriff, "I really believe the Lord has intervened with Joe and is going to give him a new beginning."

In court I got a thirty-five year sentence; it came as such a shock that my legs turned to jelly, and the only thing I felt was numb. As we left the old Gothic-revival style courthouse, a thousand questions ran dizzyingly through my mind. *Could things change? Thirty-five years was a long time. Will I have to go to the federal penitentiary later? What have I gotten myself into?* The jail was about 100 yards away from the courthouse and each step toward it felt like an eternity, as if I were walking in slow motion. I just couldn't wrap my mind around my sentence. The doors to the jail opened and I thought: *Is this* really *where I will spend the next thirty-five years of my life?* As Delight and I stood shell-shocked in the lobby, the sheriff, in God's perfect timing, walked by and noticed us standing there.

"Is that Delight?" his voice was warm. "Why don't ya'll come back to my office?"

Once we were in his office he asked me, "Are you guilty?"

"Yes sir, I'm guilty," I told him freely.

Surprised at my candor, he smiled. "Well you're the first guilty person I've ever had in my jail."

I managed to smile back at him, warming to his personable demeanor. The Lord was already giving me more strength and hope that things might work out for an early release. The sheriff told me about a drug program he was developing and asked if I wanted to volunteer. The program would enable me to talk to kids about what drugs had done to my life. There was the possibility my volunteering would help lessen my parole time. The Lord had opened a door for me to feel human again. By explaining what I was going through and helping others to avoid making the mistake I had made. He also provided the gift of not going to the federal penitentiary as long as I was participating in this program. The Lord's hands were all over this situation, and His presence was unquestionable. I eagerly told the sheriff "Yes."

Back in my cell, I was overwhelmed by everything that had happened. The sentencing had sent me into a pit of despair, but a few moments later the sheriff offered me some hope.

A week after my sentencing I got a job in the kitchen through another inmate. Joe Sedida was an older, Italian, ex-mafia guy, who liked to keep his past and his secrets to himself. Somehow we managed to be friends—probably due to the fact that we were both on the quiet side. I didn't mix or mingle with the rest of the inmates, and he was the same way, a little private and secretive. I think he noticed the fact that I didn't brag and play tough guy. Most of the other inmates were trying to impress each other with foul language and how they had lived on the outside. I didn't want any part of that, and I'm guessing Joe Sedida didn't either. He was "Big Joe" and I became "Little Joe."

After a few months of working together, Big Joe began to share with me more about his life. He had been involved in big heists with the mob, robbing large corporations and smuggling drugs. He would tell me stories about his friends in the mob, including the owner of the San Francisco 49ers. But now Big Joe was working as a baker in the jail's kitchen. His ex-partner had also been arrested and was my cellmate or "cellie" as we called them in jail. Eventually Big Joe's ex-partner was able to buy his way out of jail, but Big Joe had to serve his full time.

The job Joe helped me get as a trustee in the kitchen was a huge step up for me, both literally and figuratively— trustees got to wear tennis shoes instead of flip-flops. My feet hadn't been warm since I was arrested. It certainly wasn't hard to find humility in jail. Even though in my new job I only made about seven cents an hour, I was determined to do whatever work God put my hand to. And, I was determined to do it well. Even if I had to clean toilets, cut grass, pull weeds, or make sandwiches, I would please the Lord. By keeping my focus on him, and not my surroundings, I didn't let discouragement or pride get me down.

One evening, a church came to the jail and put on a play. This was an unusual event in the jail and I was excited to see it. The play was about Joseph and his coat of many colors. I was stunned as my mind raced back to what Doc had told me about being the reincarnated Joseph of the Bible. After the play I walked up to the actors and said, "*I* am Joseph." Once again my mind wrestled with questions about this strange power that seemed to be working in my life. I thought I had made a break with my past, but maybe there was more connection than I realized. I talked to Big Joe about it later at work. I was in prison and had befriended a baker, just like Joseph in the Bible. It was a strange spiritual correlation, but I was still confused about the spiritual realm. My work in the kitchen gave me a small sense of purpose. There were about eight other trustees that I worked with. We began at 4:30 in the morning to prepare to serve breakfast at 7:30. It took me a few days of being in the kitchen to get the swing of things, but I learned the ropes very quickly. I told them that I liked to cook and offered to scramble all of the eggs. After we cleaned up from breakfast, we'd go back to our cells for a few hours to rest or nap before it was lunch time, which was also a hot meal. Sometimes, I cooked chicken and vegetables or I made dessert. In the evening, we mostly served sandwiches. It was my job to clean the oven and the stove when we were finished cooking for the day.

The work felt good, and I took pride in my work. Miss Bobby, the lady who ran the kitchen, ran a tight ship. The kitchen was spotless. She was like a page of military code, strict and no nonsense. By contrast, Mrs. Cheney, her assistant, was a joyful older black woman, a little heavyset, an old-fashioned southern girl at heart with a beautiful spirit. She was sweet and nice to me, very open and friendly. She helped me out as I learned the ways of the kitchen. As we got to be friends, she'd bring me fish that her friends had caught so that I could cook it and have it for lunch. I had confided to her that I didn't really like to eat meat. Mrs. Cheney was one of those special people who helped me stay grounded in jail. But if you stepped out of line in Miss Bobby's kitchen, you'd be back in orange, a regular inmate again. (We got *white* suits as trustees.)

The jail cells were arranged in a space like a circle that we called pods, and as a trustee, you could go in and out of the pod without an escort. There was an exercise room that I spent a lot of time in, doing sit-ups and lifting weights.

There was also some space outside that I enjoyed. Mostly I just laid in the sun when I could.

My cellmate and I also did a Bible study together. He was an ex-biker, a big gang guy. He didn't talk much either, but we got along. We got a pamphlet with Bible questions to complete. I still wasn't able to read well, so I copied answers from him because I wanted to get a certificate that said I'd finished the Bible study. Certificates mean a lot in jail. They're the symbols of accomplishment. I was cheating, but I was getting the Word into my head.

I met Jim Proctor because I was allowed to go in and out of the pod without an escort. He was the guard for the pods, and eventually we became friends as I went through my transition. He would let me come and sit with him in the control room of the pod. He had a light in his eye, a spark. He was studying to be a priest, and one day he mentioned Jesus. We began talking about God, and Jim shared a little bit about his own life. He once had a drinking problem and was still fighting his own demons. He'd had a major collision with a tractor trailer, and they pronounced him dead at the site of the accident. But he was revived, and wanted to commit his life to the Lord after that. He went to AA meetings, and he'd been clean about 18 months when we first began talking. I felt comfortable with him, like he could relate to me. Still pondering about the play about Joseph, I asked him about reincarnation. He was the one who told me it wasn't scriptural, but I still found myself inter-mingling my ideas with truth. Even so, I was trying to listen to God.

Somehow Jim got permission from the sheriff to take Joe Sedida and me to St. Marks, this little white-painted Episcopal church about two blocks away even though I'd quit going to church in jail after the baptism segregation incident.

Since the sheriff had been so good to me, when he asked me to share my story inside the jail, I didn't hesitate. I gave my first testimony, describing my past and my desire for a new life, in a court room in the jail, and I talked for about five minutes before judges, lawyers, inmates, and some people from the community. It was a really special moment. My life was beginning to feel like it had some purpose. When you've been yanked out of society and put into jail, it turns your life upside down. It was in jail that I first found the stillness that could even allow me to listen to God. Out in the world, walking Satan's path, I was so busy with life on the streets running drugs that I had no time to listen to the still, small voice of God. This was the first time that I was forced to slow down, sit in one place, and let the Lord touch my heart. And as He did so, gradually I was finding that I could actually *love* myself. The blinders were taken away from my eyes, and everything was brand new.

Chapter 9

Redemption

My first testimony outside the jail was with a Drug Abuse Resistance Education (or DARE) program at an elementary school. I was shackled and clad in my bright orange jumpsuit, and that was the most humiliating thing I've ever gone through. The chain around my waist was connected to the cuffs around my hands and ankles; I could barely move and was only able to walk in baby steps. Shackling has a way of stripping you of your humanity, of degrading you. I'd never been more humbled than while I was on that stage in front of a couple hundred kids, trying to explain to them how I'd gotten myself in that situation and persuade them to avoid it. I think it was then that I finally realized the full price of my actions.

My second experience giving a testimony outside of jail was a few weeks later. The sheriff and I went to a high school, and thankfully, I was allowed to wear my civilian clothes. I can't describe the feeling that ran through me as I dressed that morning in my jeans, nice collared shirt, and sweater. Regular clothes lent some normalcy to my existence and gave me back some of the humanity I'd been stripped of when I was incarcerated.

As we left the high school, I noticed that while the sheriff was talking to the kids earlier, he'd somehow managed to rub against the chalkboard and get chalk on his sports jacket. Before giving it any thought, I reached out and dusted off his jacket for him. That was one of the first moments of trust and vulnerability between us. An inmate was never supposed to put his hands on a sheriff, but I had guilelessly done so, and he appreciated the gesture. We developed a good rapport, and little by little I told him about my life, but not about my reading disability. I was still very ashamed of things that had happened in my past and afraid that the sheriff might find out I wasn't a college graduate, in fact I could barely read or write. I thought the truth might hinder my chance to do these testimonies, and I grew paranoid as I hid the truth. Satan was still trying to keep me in shame of who I was. But the Lord was also working on me. He was revealing to me what it means to repent, to turn away from the past and embrace a new future. I didn't understand a lot about my new faith, but I understood what it meant to repent. I continually kept repentance, the idea of turning away from my past and toward a new direction, in my mind. I was slowly learning how to leave the distorted thinking of my past and grasp the truths of God and his Word.

During my time in the kitchen, I saw that the jail, which was new, didn't have any vinyl composition tile (VCT) on the floor. VCT is good for high-traffic areas like institutions and schools because it is relatively inexpensive yet durable and easy to maintain. So I talked to the sheriff and told him that I had a flooring company, and I knew how to install what they needed. He decided to let me install the tile. I called my old friend and boss Burt Deach and ordered the VCT for the jail. For a week, I worked on installing the tile in the evening when my work in the kitchen was through. In the end the pride I took in that job helped me to win favor with everyone.

My work in the kitchen and with different DARE programs kept me busy. One Saturday when Delight came to visit, they'd scheduled an appointment with a church's community group for us to go do a testimony about saying no to drugs and how drugs had affected our lives. The policeman that went with us, affectionately nicknamed "Big Bruce," was around 6'4 and 250 pounds, and the kids loved him! We used a confiscated hot-rod as an attention grabber for the kids, and as we rode down the road on that bright, sunny day, I was happy to have Delight with me again. This particular meeting was in a park's picnic area, and in that idyllic setting, Delight and I cried like babies as we poured our hearts out to these youth. We told them about how hard it was for us to be apart. It was a really cleansing feeling to let go of our emotions for a while.

Some of the churches I visited to share my testimony were small African American churches in the middle of the woods somewhere. It was there that the Holy Spirit really started working amazingly in my heart. They would lay hands on me, anoint my head with oil, and pray in tongues over me; the Lord used them to work on me in so many ways.

Whenever I had the chance, I went to St. Mark's, the Episcopal Church, with Jim Proctor, the guard who had taken me there originally. I met Jim's mom and dad, and occasionally after church we'd go out to lunch. The love of Christ was enveloping and overwhelming me, and I saw that it transcended reading Scripture. I'd always had a tough time trying to get to know the Lord simply by reading the Word because I couldn't read well. However, He showed me that His acceptance and pursuit of me went beyond my weaknesses. One day at St. Mark's with Jim, in a service of about fifteen people, we came to the front and they anointed us with oil and prayed for us. That day the priest told the parable of the talents from Matthew 25:14-30. I felt the Lord touch me in a powerful way with that passage. Since that moment it has resonated with me and lifted my spirit. I prayed and hoped that one day I would be able to do it the right way--take whatever talents I had and multiply them for the Lord. I wanted to do the best I could if he offered me a second chance.

It became apparent that I was becoming the sheriff's right-hand man. Every so often he'd take trips to visit his ex-wife and children. He couldn't drive very well because he had bad hips. His limp made his walk reminiscent of a penguin, and he couldn't bend over or drive comfortably for long periods of time. So he'd take me, and I'd drive giving him a break when he was tired. We talked a lot about wrestling and football, and life in general. Spending that one-on-one time with the sheriff was amazing. I discovered that he was somebody who really cared about me and was willing to give me a second chance. We spent time with his kids and sometimes went to sporting events together. His family treated me like family.

The sheriff had a boat. I'd help him put that in the water. Occasionally, we'd fish and bring the fish we caught back to feed inmates, holding down costs at the jail. Other times we'd go out to the bay, and he showed me where there were oysters, and we'd eat them right there in the boat. Or we'd take clams back to his house and make an unbelievably good clam soup. He tried to show me how to throw a fish net and pull fish out of the water, but more often than not, I'd only succeed in getting us wet! There is quite an art to pulling fish in from a net.

After a trip with the sheriff there were times that I'd go back to my cell in complete awe of God's loving kindness. *Why me?* I'd ask myself. *Why me?* It was such a privilege to have an amazing new friend as I faced a thirty-five year incarceration. I was always eager to spend time with the sheriff. If he ever needed any help with anything outside of the jail, he'd grab me, and I'd go. One Sunday, I visited a new church. I had a pastor pray and speak in tongues over me. As I stood in that circle, with their arms around me, I was struck by the sincerity and depth of how they spoke to God. It was the first time I'd ever heard anyone pray that way, and I wasn't scared, only filled with warmth. The Lord was getting to me from so many different angles.

Building bookshelves was one of the jobs that the sheriff gave Big Joe and me to do. We built about twenty-eight bookshelves. Some went into the library at the jail, some into St. Marks, and some to the Christian retreat center. They were beautiful. We cut each piece, sanded them down, and stained them, and then put on the lacquer. The whole process took around three to four months. We did all of the work at the retreat center, going out about twice a week. The retreat center was right on the bay, a beautiful, quiet spot, and I enjoyed working there. Sometimes, the sheriff would give us money to buy lunch, and we'd get to sit and eat together. On another job, Big Joe and I also put a cherry wood floor in one of the priest's main offices at St. Mark's. They eventually put up a plaque honoring the work we had done there.

I would sit back in my cell and just wonder—how did this happen to me? How could such grace be bestowed upon me? I was earning the trust and respect of the sheriff and others around me, despite being an inmate. Many times the state had tried to put me in the state prison, but the sheriff was adamant about keeping me in Woodbine. He defended me and told them I was doing the drug program, and he needed me to participate in the program.

My life was being filled with generous, trusting people who loved the Lord. As we grew closer, the sheriff had to have hip surgery in Jacksonville, and Jim Proctor took Big Joe and me down to visit him after the operation was completed. We were the first people to visit, and we got to help him stand for the first time and take his first new steps. Jim had known the sheriff since he was a young boy and really looked up to him. So, it was a precious and sacred time we were allowed to have with this man who was such a formative figure in each of our lives. When he came back to Woodbine, I'd go to his house and since he couldn't bend down, I'd help him get his socks on. I didn't feel worthy to have this bond, but I was grateful to the Lord for showing me I was worthy.

It was about six months into jail that I started fasting and praying for an early release. Each day I worked to please the Lord. I was reprogramming my way of life, and it helped me to gain strength. God was changing my life and thoughts, and as I began seriously fasting, a deeper communication with the Him began. I wasn't able to read the Scriptures well and didn't understand much in the way of theology, but I knew I could fast. I started with a day and learned how to stop eating. It is a challenge to give up earthly things in order to focus on heavenly things, but it's worth it. Even though I was still mixed up about some scriptural things, I was making a concerted effort to reach out and know the Lord. I understood that the word "repent" meant to turn away from sin and walk toward the Lord. I began to base my life on that one simple word---repent.

Even though my old life was slipping away, it was putting up a fight. I still struggled with the desire to get high, thoughts of cocaine and pot were constantly in my mind. There were several times when I gave in the craving and found a way to get high. One time I was given a hand me down sports jacket to wear to one of the outings from the jail. Inside the pocket I found a marijuana joint and as soon as I could be alone, I smoked it. Another time Delight came down to visit me, bringing a "gift" of cocaine. We paid a guard $100 to leave us alone for an hour and we used the time to get high on the coke. Even though I was making great strides in my relationship with the Lord, I still thought I could control my addiction just enough to not get in trouble or have it take over my life again.

During this time, Delight was busy doing what she could to help. She procured letters from old teachers, from Marshall Dobberman, my wrestling coach, from Dr. White, and work letters. She sent all the letters down to the sheriff in support of my appeal. Delight also managed to convince my mom that I would be coming home sooner rather than later. My mom had a contract in hand to sell the family house that she had intended to pass on to me. Delight convinced her to keep the house and wait for me to come home. Delight was tenacious!

Delight wouldn't rest until I was out of jail. A lot of people from the community that I'd given anti-drug talks to also wrote letters supporting me. The news that my dad had fallen ill with cancer also helped my plea for early release. People began to see that I wasn't a run-of-the-mill drug dealer—they knew I wanted to change my life, and eventually the sheriff persuaded the judge to believe in me as well.

I discovered my dad would do anything in the world for me, and I hoped that once I got out I could somehow begin to mend my relationship with him. He came to Georgia and went to court when they were setting my bond. He hired a lawyer, Grayson Lane, for $15,000. However Lane turned out to be a scam artist. He took the money, came to see me one time, and I thought that the more I paid, the better chances I had of getting out. I was desperate, but I would've been better off with a public defender. After Lane got his money, he wouldn't accept Delight's calls or talk about the case with her. The only other time I saw him other than our first initial visit was in court. Losing all that money was so disheartening.

The sheriff and I were standing in the back hallway of the jail when he told me my papers had come in and I would be released. After eighteen months spent in jail, I was free! I had prayed and fasted, refusing to give up hope. So many emotions swirled through me—gratefulness, humility, joy—I gave the sheriff a huge hug. Where would I have been without him?

Jim Proctor, another blessing from the Lord in my life, bought my plane ticket back to Maryland. Delight was doing the best she should could to keep money coming in. She worked in sales at the Christian-owned company Safford Lincoln Mercury, but we were still struggling. Our phone bill was almost $1500 a month and she could barely keep the electricity on. The house was old, so the roof was leaking and the back porch fell in. I had credit card debt and owed the bank $30,000. So, it was truly a huge blessing that Jim bought my plane ticket. Delight and I would start our new life in the red, but the Lord would bring us back step by step.

I was elated. The Lord knew it was my time, and he would teach me how to avoid falling back into drugs. His loving kindness was so overwhelming in Woodbine. I was positive it would continue to be so throughout my life. What I didn't know was that the attacks on my life weren't over yet. Woodbine had nurtured me, but I was getting ready to leave the nest and try to fly on my own.

There were several things I set my mind to doing once I got out of jail: find work, find a church, marry Delight, and spend as much time as possible with my ailing father. Finding work isn't an easy task for an ex-con, but I was blessed to have some friends from home that trusted me and would help me out.

I'd contacted my old friend Burt Deach, who I'd met early on in my drug career when I was laying carpet. He was the biggest carpet guy in town. But when the economy took a downturn and the first recession struck in the early 1980's, Burt went bankrupt. He went from having four or five big stores to having no money at all. As we sold carpet together, I learned a lot from him, and we learned to trust each other. I could only hope that my time in jail hadn't changed that.

While I was waiting to hear back from Burt about working for him and also waiting for my parole papers to come from Georgia, I found a temporary job with my neighbor, Big George. I'd known George since I was three years old. He was a builder and owned a construction company, so it was easy to get a job with him as a laborer. For $7 an hour, three to four times a week I did manual labor, mostly cleaning up the jobs and anything that still needed to be done. It was hard work, but it felt good to be making an honest living.

Working with George reminded me of the other people who had helped me along the way, specifically Rowdy. I owed him a visit to thank him after what he'd done for Delight and me. The familiar roads downtown reminded me of my old life. Internally a struggle was raging, another spiritual battle for my life. I knew that being in the house with Rowdy was risky—what if the police came in and arrested me again? On top of my fears, my desire to get high again was stronger than ever. I had battled it in jail constantly, but now I was back in my old territory, among the familiar surroundings of my past life. I knew I was being haunted by my past. That day my past showed how strong a hold it still had on me and on my way out, I asked Rowdy for a joint. He hesitated, but gave one to me with a funny look as if to say, "Here we go again." I took it, thinking that it couldn't hurt just to get high one more time. Pot wasn't as dangerous as cocaine, was it?

I smoked that joint on the drive home. I'd never felt so bad, or so guilty about smoking before. I started to realize that I was a different person now, a new person. The old Joe who used to be able to smoke a joint without a second thought was slipping away. I haven't seen Rowdy since that day. I had to cut my ties with anyone who would lead me down that path. My flesh was trying to control my spirit, and all of my friends were waiting for me to come out of "retirement." Nobody around me fully trusted that the Lord had touched my heart and blessed me so deeply. They were all waiting and watching to see what I would do. I found out later that after Rowdy sent the money for bail, he'd come to the house, expecting "repayment" from Delight— repayment in the only form a woman with no money could give. I was deeply disheartened to hear about what he tried. When I was able to, I sent him $1,000 to pay what I owed him.

Since I had committed my whole life to the Lord, He wanted every area of my life to honor Him. I knew that there was one area that He wanted me to change. I needed to marry Delight and accept the full responsibility of marriage as God intended. Delight was really convicted about how a relationship should be. We were living together and I knew that it was time to step up to the plate and marry the girl who went to bat for me. We wanted to live in the light as the Lord wanted us to. Delight was estranged from her family, her brothers especially. She had her own demons to fight just as I did. And for me, everyone was holding their breath, thinking I was going to be back into the mental hospital or jail. They weren't exactly compassionate after everything I'd put the family through for years, and I didn't blame them. So we decided to go back to Woodbine, where I'd felt my first real sense of family and community in Christ. I was captured by the peace I had felt in that community and wanted it in my new life with Delight.

We called St. Mark's and booked a date. The sheriff gave Delight away and Jim Proctor was my best man. Mrs. Proctor was the matron of honor, and they put on a beautiful little wedding. There were about thirty people there—the sheriff's family, some people from town. The Proctor's had a condo on St. Simon's island in Florida that they let us use for our honeymoon. The sheriff gave us a few hundred dollars since we were broke to spend on our trip. We played golf and went out to dinners; it was a great time. Enjoying my new freedom, however, came with thoughts of cocaine—the drug that had been my "friend" for many years. That idea was my constant companion during our honeymoon on St. Simon's. Cocaine had been a large part of me up until then, and I couldn't shake the feeling that without it, something was missing. I still didn't know Satan was my enemy and he was stalking me, ready to devour me all over again. A voice kept nagging me, goading me, pounding me to give cocaine another chance.

Chapter 10

A Second Chance

I knew that once we got back to Maryland from our honeymoon, there would be a lot of new responsibilities now that I had a wife. Finding a job after being incarcerated might not be that easy. I decided that it wouldn't hurt anything if Delight and I used some cocaine before starting fresh again in Maryland. I arranged for someone in Maryland to send some cocaine down to my hideout with Barry in Florida so we could get high on our way home from St. Simon's. I thought Barry's was a place where I could try it again without getting into trouble. The desire was so strong to get to Barry's that it was on my mind constantly; it had captured me. Satan was by my side, talking to my flesh, making me feel as though I needed the physical sensations that cocaine could give me.

So after the honeymoon since my parole papers still hadn't come in yet, we drove down to Ft. Lauderdale to Barry's trailer where he had cocaine waiting. Without wasting much time, we both used the cocaine and got high. Immediately my personality changed, her personality changed, and I felt all the frustration, confusion, and hurt that I'd worked so hard to relinquish come flooding back. The cocaine ushered us right back into the demonic realm and it made us miserable. I hated what we became when we used. I knew it would lead me down a dark road and I didn't want to lead Delight down it with me. I knew I needed to take a stand and resist the pull back to that life.

On the way back from Ft. Lauderdale we stopped in Woodbine, Georgia. I felt so ashamed that I'd let myself and the sheriff down. While we were there, I got a call from Maryland saying my parole papers had shown up and my parole officer wanted to see me as soon as we got back. The hair on the back of my neck stood up. It felt like electricity shot down my spine. My worst nightmare had been realized. I knew that I would have to take a drug test as soon as I got back. The cocaine in my system would certainly show up and put my new found freedom at risk.

I finally realized that all the struggles and challenges throughout my life were part of a war by Satan for my soul. If I didn't stay committed, I knew he would crush me. I had to take a stand against Satan or he would destroy me. As Delight and I were driving back, I was trying to think of all the things I could do to pass the urine test. I realized that I'd risked my freedom in Christ and with my new family, and that Satan had tricked me into using drugs again. All of my shame and all that guilt that was woven into my life before came rushing back.

When we got back I was afraid to go home, so we stayed in a hotel. I told my officer that we were having problems getting back. I got on a bus and stayed with my mom for four days, and Delight went back to Maryland. What a traumatic experience to go through right after our marriage! It certainly wasn't the way we wanted to start our marriage off. I waited as long as I could at my mom's because I wanted to make sure the cocaine was out of my system. I promised myself then that I would never, ever do cocaine again. I would not risk losing all the love, joy, and freedom I was experiencing by falling prey to Satan's tricks. With all the strength within me, with the strength of Christ, I put my foot down to crush Satan's stronghold. I would take a firm stand against Satan. I would win the battle. I had Christ with me this time, and I knew I wanted to choose love and life, not death. Since that moment, I was drug free, because of the power of Christ within me.

When I went to see my parole officer, amazingly, she didn't administer the urine test. I could start my life over! Step by step, things were changing for me. I had been given another chance, once again.

Several months went by as I settled into my new life and new routines, enjoying the hard, but honest work with

Big George's construction company. I was committed to change, but Delight was still struggling with her own demons. She loved the Lord, but she was finding it hard to let go of the old life. I knew that it was even more important for me to stay strong because I knew the struggles Delight had.

After we got back from our honeymoon, one of the first things Delight wanted to do was buy a boat, a cabin cruiser to be exact. Without my knowledge, she signed for a loan. Although it was a great deal, we were still flat broke. I was so upset and couldn't believe that she would do that without telling me. Somehow or another, she convinced me to go look at the boat, and once I saw it, I was so impressed that my common sense flew out the window. I got caught up in the moment and caved in. I hated conflict anyway, so I let it go. We took the boat to another marina closer to home, and I figured we'd deal with it later.

One night that summer we took some friends out for a ride. Delight was drinking, trying to have a good time, and gradually her mood turned from jovial, to sour, to downright nasty. The demons showed up, and it scared me that she would be so rude to our friends on the boat. The experience shook Delight and she vowed to quit drinking, and finally I thought we had put that part of our life behind us.

Later in the summer the sheriff and his family came up to visit and we took them out on the boat to Annapolis. I'm sure he wondered whether I was dealing again since we now owned this boat. I even joked with him that I was using it to pick up bales of marijuana. But the sheriff could see that my life was different, not perfect, but I hadn't gone back to my old ways. Despite the good times on the boat, after a few months we realized we couldn't afford it or the gas it took to get across the bay. We had also stopped going to church on Sundays so that we could spend time on the boat. I knew this wasn't right. We eventually sold it for just about what we paid for it. Yes, the Lord was looking out for us again.

After the fiasco of the boat, Delight began to push for having a baby. I wanted a child, but I didn't want to bring a child into the world that would have to go through the same kinds of things that we did as children. When Delight drank, I was reminded that raising a child in that environment wouldn't be right. The doctors told her she needed to have an operation before she would be able to conceive so she had it done. I still didn't think that having a child would be a good idea, but we didn't have the kind of healthy relationship where we could talk about things and try to work through them. I desperately wanted this time in our life to be a time of change for *both* of us. I knew I'd been given a second chance and I wanted Delight to follow the Lord and His ways as much as I was.

About a year after I got out of jail, Delight's mother moved in with us, and that turned into a really tough situation. Her mother claimed to be a Christian, but she was addicted to a pain pump and took pain pills. One night I was at a Christian concert, and I got a call from Montgomery General Hospital. Delight and a girlfriend were there trying to admit Delight's mom into the psychiatric ward. Once I got there, I discovered that Delight and her mom had gotten into a huge fight, and they were still fighting, even at the hospital. I found out later that Delight and her friend had been drinking when Delight's mom claimed that Delight had stolen some of her pain pills. This started a huge fight. Eventually Delight and her friend wrapped her mom in blankets and took her to the hospital hoping to have her admitted. As I listened to them hurl hurtful accusations at one another, I couldn't help thinking that Delight was paying her mom back for all the years of abuse and neglect she'd endured. As they were fighting, Delight's mom denounced her and told her she was out of the will, that she'd never receive her inheritance.

Before her mother had come to live with us, Delight

had worked hard to clean up a family mess. She was trying to help her mother sell a house that her brother had owned. It had been confiscated by the DEA. After her brother was busted for his cocaine stash and growing pot on the property, he fled the country, and Delight stepped in. She put a lot of work into that house—cleaning, painting, and repairs. In the end, the family only got mad that Delight kept some of the money in payment for the work she put into the house. It was the same family that had refused to send money to bail Delight out of jail when we were arrested. Delight wanted a connection with her family, but the dysfunction and on-going abuse were too great. It broke Delight's heart, and it was a painful thing to watch unfold.

Watching Delight's family made me realize that part of the change I'd wanted to enact in my life needed to include developing a better relationship with my mom and dad. I began working on this when the Lord gave me my early release. I knew my dad didn't have long to live because of his cancer, so I tried to spend as much time as I could with him during his last year of life. That time was such a precious gift.

I loved my dad. Even if he hadn't learned how to communicate well, or how to love my mom well, he'd always been supportive of me, kind, and giving. He just couldn't completely break free from the cycles of hurt and violence that he'd endured as child. Despite his emotional distance, Dad had prayed for me for years. Sometimes he would show me articles in papers about people getting busted to influence me, but he never tried to stop me. He did throw out a stash of cocaine I had been keeping at his trailer in Ocean City, however he never confronted me directly about it. He knew the kind of lifestyle I had led with drugs and loved me still the same.

Dad liked to write poetry even though he'd been a military man. He saw a tremendous amount of evil things during WWII as a deep-sea diver. The only incident he ever spoke to me about had occurred after Pearl Harbor and there were hundreds of bodies in the sea. Dad, as a deep-sea diver, was enlisted to help raise the sunken ships up from where they'd fallen so the military could get the ships out of the Harbor. In preparation for this, a model of a ship was taken and turned upside down so that the divers could learn how to go into the ship upside down and walk to the hull. Once the divers reached the hull, they were supposed to attach tanks there and fill the tanks with air so they could raise the ship out of the water. But Dad soon realized that mock dives could not have prepared him for what he'd actually encounter. It was oily and mucky with debris floating everywhere. There was little visibility. But to my dad's horror, he *could* see the dead bodies he'd need to walk through to reach the bow of the ship. It was a terrifying and gruesome experience that he went through for our freedom. These experiences would stick with him and affect the way he would bring up his children and how he communicated. I can only imagine all the pain and trauma he carried and never talked about it. Now, as an adult I see that, but when I was growing up I couldn't. Regardless of all of the misery we went through together,-- misery he'd caused, misery I'd caused—in the end we found a deep love for each other. We were closer because now I was walking with Christ, and it opened my heart to him.

I really cherished the time I got to spend with him. He was in a nursing home, and Delight and I would visit him three or four times a week. We'd go to McDonalds where he loved to get a fish sandwich, or I'd bring him crab soup from a local restaurant he liked. Sometimes we'd watch the Redskins and talk about the game. I was blessed to have this time with him and I was grateful to the Lord for each moment.

One evening, close to dusk, Delight and I were driving down Georgia Avenue, about ten minutes away from the nursing home. We passed the exit for the nursing home, and all of the sudden I told her that we needed to turn around to see him, so we did. I had such a strong sense that I needed to do this. It was as if the Holy Spirit told me to turn around. Dad wasn't doing very well that day. He had pneumonia and had lost a lot of weight. I knew his time here was coming to an end soon. The next morning, my sister called to tell me Dad had died.

I could've been in jail and missed those special times with my dad. Even though I was thirty-eight years old before we ever hugged and kissed, it was worth it. In the nursing home I told him I loved him, and he told me he loved me. We kissed each other's cheeks. Those moments were full of redemption and grace. I had to grow up for that to be able to happen and the Lord brought maturation so I could enjoy that last year of relationship with Dad.

He never told me while he was living, but at his funeral, the pastor showed us his Bible bearing a date that showed when he'd given his life to the Lord. Apparently, it had happened while I was in jail. Delight and I were deeply comforted by this.

While I was building our father-son relationship, Delight and I had found a church to call home. We'd been all over town hunting for a church, and we remained open-minded as we searched. We went to black churches, white churches, Pentecostal churches, Episcopal churches. We tried everything. In the end, we found Montgomery Community Church and their pastor, Clem. An old drug friend of mine had also turned his life over to the Lord, and he invited us to Montgomery Church, a small church with about 100-150 people. While doing some carpet work at the church, I discovered that I really liked the pastor, so Delight and I settled into church life there.

One day, Clem asked me to go for a drive with him. As we were driving around in the car Clem asked me if I'd given my life to the Lord, and I said no, not verbally. So we pulled into the parking lot of a little tavern down from the church, and we prayed. That day I accepted the Lord as we prayed together. The Holy Spirit came over me, my body shook, and I almost lost my speech. It was an incredible moment. Clem took us under his wing and began to teach us about the Lord. He would come to our house at 6am to study the Bible with us. His commitment to helping us grow showed us a lot about what it meant to be committed to the Lord. Eventually Delight and I were baptized and gave our lives fully over to the Lord. My sister Pam, her husband, and many of our neighbors came to see me get baptized. They had faithfully prayed for me for years while I had lived my wild life. Delight and I were really encouraged to grow in our faith by the church, so we decided to make that church our church home. The Lord allowed me to use some of my talents from my past to work in the church's sound ministry. I also began going to the men's breakfast hosted there and eventually became part of the team that organized the event. Hoping to share the peace I had found in Christ, I invited many of my friends to come to the breakfast.

Delight got involved with the children's ministry, and her drinking disappeared for a short time. It was the happiest I'd seen her in a long while. We also went to a Bible study, and at least once a month, I'd fast for a day or sometimes two days. That was my own private way of thanking the Lord and staying focused, and not letting the demonic realm or my past pull me away. Beyond going to church on Sunday, fasting was a personal practice I continued. Unfortunately, despite how comfortable Clem had made me feel, I still felt like an alien, like I had no one to relate to, and I couldn't be myself. I still had so much shame and hurt from my past that I hadn't dealt with. I didn't have a clue about how to face it. It had only been about a year since my release, and it is tough readjusting to life on the outside and re-learning how to fit in with society.

By the end of my first year outside of jail, I had met many of my goals. I'd married Delight, restored my relationship with my Dad, and found steady, satisfying work. Burt Deach had agreed to give me a chance and I worked with him at his company, Carpet Decorators, as a shop foreman. I was grateful to have a job. I placed bids, helped cut carpet, did repair work and installation. I did a little bit of everything for him. I ran a million dollar job for Burt for a huge twelve story building in which I measured and cut the carpet and managed the crews, all for $9 an hour. Burt lent me the money to get my first car out of jail. He was a shrewd businessman, and had grown wealthy again as the years went on after the recession.

During this time I was slowly proving to my family and friends that this new life was real and that I could earn a living without drugs in my life. In particular, my relationship with my mother began to grow as she saw me walking the straight path, and I got my feet on the ground. My mom called me her "walking miracle." About this time, Mom decided that she was going to write her inheritance papers. She decided to leave money to my two sisters and leave the property we had grown up on to me. Although my sisters weren't so sure of my new life, my mom believed that I would make something of the property and needed it to move forward in my life with Delight.

Once my mom released the property to us we were able to get a loan from the bank, using the house as collateral. One of the first things Delight and I did was pay off our credit cards. We also got some appliances for the little house we were living in on the property and fixed the leaky roof. We also took the old recording studio, demolished it, and turned it into a rental unit to help pay back the loan we'd just received. It was important to us to settle our past debts as well as put ourselves on firm footing for the future.

After three years of working for Burt, he wanted me to go on salary. However, I wasn't getting paid that much, and I didn't want to have to go out and become a salesman for him, I turned him down. He'd given me so much confidence, but I was still insecure about my abilities. Burt had never looked down on me because I was dyslexic. He never assumed I couldn't do something. He taught me a lot about how to run a business. Burt trusted me and even though he didn't understand my new found faith he was happy that it worked for me.

I never had to stray far from home to find work. Drew Wilson was the little brother of three guys, Carter, Brian, and Gil who were on the wrestling team with me in high school while I'd been captain. They had always been good to me. It turned out that Drew had a cabinet shop about three miles from my house, so I did a couple flooring jobs for him as he remodeled kitchens. I sold him some vinyl floors and got some guys to put it in, and Drew was happy with the work, so he let me begin developing a flooring division as part of his company. Delight helped to keep my books for the flooring work I was developing, while she was still working at the car dealership.

I put all my energy into my fledgling floor division at Drew's, doing kitchen floors, hardwood, and selling carpet. The friends who I had developed business relationships with at Carpet Decorators with Burt also helped me out at Drew's, and before I knew it, I had about $225,000 in sales, which grossed me about $26,000 after Drew took his profits.

Just as my new life was beginning to truly take shape, my past came back, threatening to steal what the Lord had given me. The sheriff was up for re-election in Woodbine and powerful enemies were trying to get him out of office. In a TV interview, he commented about local judges and lawyers trying to take advantage of their power over inmates, coercing the inmates into more illegal activities using bribes or intimidation. He wanted to stop those officials from taking confiscated drug money for themselves when the money was meant to be used for public good. These judges and lawyers retaliated by attempting to arrest the sheriff through a Georgia Bureau of Investigation (GBI) sting operation on him. An FBI officer from Maryland called me every four or five days and asked me questions about the sheriff. The GBI thought the sheriff brought me confiscated drugs to sell for him. Eventually, an agent said he wanted to interview me. He said, "You don't *have* to come see me...but I think you'd better come see me." He knew there was a chance I would be sent back to jail. He had a bold, cocky attitude. This was a tough time for me, especially as I was trying to build trust with people on my job and even my own family. It's hard to shake the image of "convict" and this certainly wasn't helping. The FBI thought they could break me, but there was nothing for them to find. Bill Smith's friendship had always been just that—friendship, with nothing on the side.

With the feds involved and anxious to speak with me, Mom's remarriage to the well-connected Donahoe family came in handy. They had political ties with the FBI in Washington so she called them to see if she could get any information on what was happening with the sheriff and me. They told Mom that if I didn't cooperate and act as a "good" witness for the case I'd go back to jail. Now I knew I had to get a lawyer I trusted. Joe Valerio knew his stuff; he was in the House of Delegates at Annapolis in Maryland, and I'd been connected with him since my younger, wilder days. He'd helped get me out of the mental hospital. I went to him for advice back then, and he seemed to be the perfect person to call for my situation now.

I met the FBI officer in Valerio's office. This was the same officer who had been calling me and threatening me to cooperate with the investigation. This particular officer had a chip on his shoulder. Self-righteous and cocky, Delight could sense the vibes he threw off right away. A tough guy, he blustered into the room in cowboy boots and a suit, and his arrogance was infuriating. He knew he was right before we even spoke, no matter what the situation might've been. Since this was my second interrogation, I was familiar with the questions, and I wasn't going to offer any information that they could use against the sheriff. I was nervous but I felt confident. For the first time in my life I hadn't done anything wrong. It was a nerve-wracking experience, even with as much faith as I had in the Lord. As the meeting went on I relaxed. Feeling the Lord's presence allowed me to speak openly and honestly. I told the officer my testimony of faith, how Jesus had helped me through Bill Smith. I told him that I considered the sheriff a good friend because he'd shown me the love of Christ.

That's when the officer, stunned, said, "There's no way a sheriff could be friends with an ex-con."

I smiled to myself. This officer obviously didn't know what the Lord could do.

A grand jury summons was inevitable, and I was subpoenaed. The FBI flew me down to North Carolina and got me a hotel. Delight was afraid they would put me back in jail and that I wasn't coming home. My mom, on the advice of the Donahoes, helped me procure another lawyer down there. When I met this lawyer, I told him all about turning my life over to the Lord and my friendship with the sheriff. And even he pulled me aside and said, "Now tell me the real truth. What are you and the sheriff *really* doing? How much cocaine is he giving you?" It was hard for anyone to believe my story, but I stood by the truth. I was there for two or three days, waiting while several other people went before the grand jury. As it turned out they didn't want my testimony in the courtroom. *Why*, I wondered. In the end the sheriff was acquitted of all charges.

I returned home, but a few weeks later Delight and I went back down to visit him. At this time the sheriff was in the midst of a re-election campaign, so we joined in to help him out. The elections were held while we were there, and the sheriff was re-elected! After seeing him in handcuffs only a few weeks earlier, it was wonderful to see our friend vindicated.

Chapter 11

Rebuilding: God's Way

Things in the cabinet shop were growing steadily and I wanted to work out a deal with Drew to go fifty-fifty, but he wanted 51 percent ownership of the business. I managed all the flooring work and that was half of the business, so I didn't think his offer was fair. Drew and I were friends, but he didn't want to give up control over his business, so we couldn't work things out. It made sense to me that he would want to maintain ownership, but I needed something more. I realized I had finally gained enough self-confidence to strike out on my own in business.

So Delight and I prayed with Pastor Clem about going into business for ourselves. It was really important to us to have that pastoral support. We didn't want to make a move without God's provision and blessing. I'd saved up about $26,000 from my work at the cabinet shop, and it seemed like a mountain of money for us at the time.

Despite the challenges that we could face, in 1993, Delight and I decided to start our own carpet business, Craftmasters Interiors. One of our main problems was our lack of credit. We needed a loan, but had no track record to prove we had a viable company. It had been almost four years since I'd gotten out of jail. I had worked hard, honored God, and gradually gained the trust of my friends again. It was only because I had been faithful and diligent that the Lord was able to bless me with the resources we needed to start our company. Before going to a bank to get a loan, I needed to gather together some money to show we were serious about investing in our company, and I needed to show that we had work contracts already in place. The Lord provided both.

First, I went to several friends to borrow money so that we could get started. I went to Drew, my former boss. He still owed me my sales commission from the previous year. He didn't have the money he owed me to pay me up front, and told me he'd pay me as the money came in. Chuck Small, one of my first bosses that I did plumbing for when I was sixteen, loaned me $15,000 and said I could pay him back as Drew paid me. To run the business we needed about $50,000 to pay for inventory and get setup in the office to run our first job. Bill and Chris, my friends from high school, lent me $5,000 each when I told them about our dilemma. Bill and Chris told me that they thought I deserved a second chance. They knew all about my past, and they believed that I was changed by God's power.

Craftmasters Interiors would never have gotten off the ground if it also hadn't been for my friend, Dave Mensh. Dave was a property manager at several locations where I had done carpet repair when I worked for Burt. He had been impressed with my work, and we had taken a liking to each other. The first time we met, he even helped me tear out some carpet in a building, despite being in a suit and tie! Dave had just started his own real estate development company with his friend Richard and gave me the contract to install carpet in a new set of condominiums he was building. He also knew about my past but was still willing to give me a chance.

We never thought the locally owned, conservative Sandy Spring bank would give us a loan. But with $25,000 and a carpet installation contract in hand, the bank agreed to match our money. We were blessed. Right away we had the big job from Dave Mensh, installing carpet in a new apartment building. To get the contract, we had to bid against big companies. In order to compete we had to bid $8.75 per yard with pad installed—when it cost me $9 a yard to install. We wouldn't make any money if they went with the standard builders' grade carpet. We prayed we would get upgrades on the job to make money. It was a gamble. Our first client went with standard carpet, but most units at that job upgraded so we made $3 or $4 a yard on every yard that was sold. There was approximately 175 yards per unit, and there were 149 units. The first and the last unit were the base grade carpet, but everybody else upgraded. That was how we got the business rolling. That first job lead the way to forming our company, and I trusted God's guidance the whole way.

Our office was in our two bedroom house—the house I grew up in. We soon realized that my former 10x10 foot bedroom wouldn't be a large enough office to support the growing business. Eventually we dug out the basement of the house and made that into our offices. Joe Washington, a friend since kindergarten, volunteered his time to help me. We had to put new beams in from where the termites had eaten through and we jacked the house up approximately six inches. The house was creaking, and I didn't know if it could take the strain. I thought it might fall! But the house remained, and we had our new offices.

Each and every thing we accomplished, big or small, was such blessing. There was a sense of satisfaction and fulfillment that only the Lord can bring when He's working in your life. We were gradually building a solid reputation in our industry and getting work from more and more businesses. Our clients knew that I always kept my word and could be trusted. I was also staying faithful through fasting and prayer. Delight and I were learning to work together. She was a tenacious and fearless worker, and I was so grateful to have her by my side. I was amazed by how incredibly blessed we were and how the Lord was answering my prayers.

Delight and I had a nice life for a little while with our involvement in church and work. However, slowly I would come to see that making the choice to turn your life over to the Lord isn't enough. You may have the best intentions in the world. If you don't deal with the core issues that drive you into dysfunction, you still can't live in the freedom Christ has for your life.

Delight had started taking fen-phen, a popular weight

loss drug at the time, and she was drinking on top of the drug. On her birthday she invited about 80-100 people from church to the house for a barbecue. But, she never made it out of the bedroom. Everyone wondered where she was and what was happening. It was a shocking incident. I realized then that I could no longer deny that Delight was addicted to fen-phen and alcohol.

I told Delight's doctor what was going on, and she only suggested that Delight take a lower dose of fen-phen. Later, after Delight had a heart palpitation, she learned that it could be from the fen-phen. So she quit taking it. However, the drinking continued.

For the next several years things seemed to be going great and the future looked promising. The sheriff's troubles were over. Craftmasters was growing. Delight and I were enjoying the community of our church. What I didn't know was that this peace was really an uneasy truce and a new war was getting ready to break out again. This time the war would not be between me and my addictions, but Delight and hers.

It was the spring of 1998 when I received a phone call: "Mr. Tarasuk, your wife has been involved in a car accident." Delight's car was clipped from behind and she was forced over the curb and into a tree. The accident occurred three miles from our house, so when I got the phone call, my sister Pam, who lived up the street, and I both jumped in the car and sped down to the accident site. The radiator in the car had burst, and the fleece Delight wore was soaked in anti-freeze, but thankfully she had suffered no broken bones. She'd bumped her head, but the doctors sent her home and told her to rest. I was relieved to hear that Delight's injuries seemed minor and she would recover quickly.

We had a lot going on in our life. We had subdivided our property and had just begun building the first of three houses on the lots. In addition, the business was growing so quickly that we needed to hire office help. Delight and I were even considering adopting a child. I knew things were tough, but I was confident that we would come out on top if nothing got in our way. Little did I know what lay ahead for us.

The trouble started as Delight began suffering from chronic pain. The source of her pain couldn't be determined and the doctors could only recommend swimming and some mild pain medication as a way to relieve her discomfort. I installed a pool at our house, hoping it would help, but Delight rarely used it. Then one day she had a conversation with a friend who told her about Reflex Sympathetic Dystrophy Syndrome (RSDS). Delight's friend suggested that Delight might have RSDS and stressed how bad RSDS is on your nerves. Delight grabbed onto that and became convinced RSDS was causing her pain. She finally managed to convince her doctors to prescribe stronger pain medication. They prescribed OxyContin. While this brought relief it brought something else as well. After using OxyContin for several months, Delight's doctor changed her dosage to avoid problems with this powerful narcotic. Delight, however, was already addicted and believed she needed stronger medication to combat her pain. She returned to cocaine and alcohol. I knew something wasn't right, but thought it was just the effects of the pain medication. One day I came home unexpectedly and caught Delight snorting coke. I was stunned. Cocaine, my enemy, was back in my home. If my parole officer found out I could be sent back to jail. It had been six months since the accident, when this crisis occurred.

But the Lord has a way of using our crises as catalysts for change in our lives. After I discovered Delight's drug use, we began seeing a Christian psychiatrist, Dr. Kim, who promised to help manage her pain without the use of narcotics. She prescribed some medicine to help even out Delight's mood swings since she was going through tremendous depression. Dr. Kim gave us hope, and it seemed we were getting back on track.

It certainly seemed that life was still moving forward according to our plans. Many of our dreams were coming true as Craftmasters continued to grow and provide financial security for us. When I was in jail, I had let sink into my heart the scriptures about using your talents for the Lord as a means of receiving His blessing. I had tried ever since to always give my utmost, believing that He would bless it.

That's how I built my business and watched it grow over the years. Delight and I also had a dream of developing our property. She had worked tirelessly to subdivide the land into three plots. Our dream was to build a house on each lot, sell them after a few years, and use the profit to build the next house. That dream was starting to unfold now as well. We finished building our first house in the spring and moved in with the help of our church. Our former house became a rental along with the other rental we'd had for several years.

Beneath the surface, however, things weren't so stable. Delight refused to follow the advice of Dr. Kim and switched doctors to continue her OxyContin use. She was also pursuing a lawsuit against the woman who had caused her car accident. I knew Delight wasn't being fully honest in the lawsuit. And, because of that she wouldn't allow me to speak with the lawyers, or be a part of the lawsuit in any way. Four years later when the case finally went to trial, her doctors would not come to testify on her behalf. They were not willing to testify that the OxyContin they prescribed her were medically necessary. Eventually, Delight lost the case but did receive a small settlement for workman's compensation.

Delight's continuing addiction strained our relationship. It felt like we were at the end of our rope. I was falling into the trap of co-dependency, believing that I could fix Delight if I just said or did the right thing. I was sure that I could solve this problem. But my own issues were becoming apparent too. I was unable to confront. I was afraid to communicate my feelings. I was ashamed of my past. I was bound up in fear and insecurity. We *both* needed help.

In 1999 after being at Montgomery Community Church for about ten years, we heard about Cedar Ridge Community Church, where Brian McLaren was the pastor. It was only about five minutes away from the house, and with Delight now in a wheelchair because of her pain, attending Cedar Ridge made traveling to and from church much easier. It was a community oriented church that attracted many new believers as well as people simply investigating Christianity. As a "seeker" oriented church, it was non-threatening and very welcoming. After Delight and I began attending, I wanted to find a way to reach out to people too, so I started doing a men's breakfast there. I continued fasting. I also gave out pamphlets for the breakfast while at church, inviting men to come. There were three or four men I knew who weren't going to church, and I found it easier to invite them to the breakfast—the atmosphere was a little more nonthreatening. One of my friends started his walk with the Lord at Cedar Ridge's small welcoming community.

After about a year of attending Cedar Ridge, I still believed at this point that we were on the right track. Maybe we'd had a few set-backs, but at least Delight was not taking drugs. My denial was shattered one day when we went to visit my mom in Ocean City, Maryland. We stopped along the way so Delight could get a cup of coffee. After nearly an hour of waiting for her in the car with our two dogs, I went into the shopping center to find her. She wasn't in any of the stores. Increasingly worried, I asked a woman coming out of the restroom if she had seen a woman in there. Just then, Delight came out of the restroom. She finally confessed to snorting cocaine. She was buying it from some of the men who worked for us, adding money to their paychecks to pay for it. Once again, I was stunned and hurt.

That weekend was a huge reality check for us. Delight spent the weekend at my mom's house drinking and getting high. Nothing I could say or do would stop her. Throughout the three hour trip home, Delight spewed curses and angry accusations at me. I could feel the presence of an evil and dark spirit with us as we drove. She was like a woman possessed. When we returned home, she threatened suicide, further convincing me that she needed immediate help. I took her to Montgomery General, our local hospital, where they admitted her. When I returned home to collect her clothes I was shocked by what I found. Hidden in her closets and drawers were bottle after bottle of alcohol. What had happened to my wife? How had this happened without my knowing?

This crisis, just as the first one, became a catalyst for change and for the Lord to work in our lives. It was after this crisis that Delight finally agreed to go with me to get counseling. Dr. Kim introduced us to a therapist, Mary Kay Isaacs at Church of the Redeemer. Mary Kay couldn't believe that I hadn't been through any type of program since my background involved so many drugs. She suggested we work through Celebrate Recovery, a Christian recovery program founded by John Baker out of Saddleback Church in southern California. There was a group meeting at Church of the Redeemer, and we tentatively decided to give it a chance.

Ten years after jail, I'd never been through any drug program. I'd made a stand against Satan, but I wasn't free. I thought that if I stopped doing drugs, I had recovered. I thought I was healed. But I didn't realize there was so much more to freedom than that. I thought I was going to Celebrate Recovery for Delight. After all, *she* was the one with the problems, not me. I didn't do drugs anymore, so I didn't think I needed any kind of recovery program—I was on track with the Lord. But in church I continued to feel like an alien, and I couldn't share about my past. I was still carrying the shame of my dyslexia and sexual abuse. I didn't realize that I could get free from that.

When we showed up for Celebrate Recovery the first time, we sat in the parking lot of Church of the Redeemer, afraid to go in. We worked up the nerve to go up to the door, but we just couldn't make ourselves do it. However, I was desperate to turn everything over to the Lord. I wanted relief from the misery that we were both going through. So I made another commitment to the Holy Spirit.

"Lord," I said, "do whatever you can with me."

Yet again, I found myself turning it all over to Him.

We left that first night. The next week we made it through the doors of Celebrate Recovery. Delight was still in a wheelchair, and so I wheeled her in, and we stayed. I made another commitment---to do whatever I needed to do in order to be a better man for Delight. No matter how scary or shameful it might be, I knew I needed to get free so I could help her more. In my mind Delight was the one with all the problems, and I was just there for her.

For weeks in the group I would tremble and shake; I was afraid to talk. I was afraid to be around other men in small groups. Craig Brown, the leader, was especially supportive of me though, and one night I took the plunge. I was the first man to share that I'd been sexually abused when I was young. It was like a huge load of bricks had been lifted from my shoulders. After I shared, it gave other men the courage to share. The Lord used what I'd been carrying around for forty years to free not only me, but others as well. It was clear that by listening to the Holy Spirit's urging and coming clean from my past, I helped open the door of healing for myself as well as the other men in the group. Several weeks later I gave my testimony at the Cedar Ridge men's breakfast with Craig there, and it was the beginning of freedom.

I went through the same process with my dyslexia. I learned to turn over the shame and discover who I was in Christ. I couldn't have made it through this time of painful necessary sharing, if it hadn't been for the support of my

Celebrate Recovery men's group, as well as Craig and Mary Kay.

Along with turning new areas of my past over to the Lord, I also had to learn to turn my present over to him. I had been desperately trying to fix Delight on my own. I had to learn to give her to the Lord and allow Him to dictate her journey of healing. I couldn't heal her; I couldn't make her choose differently. I had to focus on my own healing, and trust the Lord to do His work in Delight's life.

Chapter 12

Facing Spiritual Battles

We were in Celebrate Recovery for six or seven months before I wanted to start a Celebrate Recovery program at Cedar Ridge. Brian, the pastor, was very encouraging, and tried to help open doors to get the ministry started there. He also suggested that we go to Saddleback Church in California and attend the 2001 Celebrate Recovery Summit.

At the time, I was afraid to leave Delight alone for longer than a few hours. Although she was attending Celebrate Recovery with me, she was still using narcotics regularly. I wasn't sure that I could go away for four days. I also wasn't sure if I could afford a plane ticket to California since things were financially tight. As I prayed about what to do, I noticed an airline voucher pinned to the bulletin board in my office. About a year earlier, Delight and I had been bumped off a flight and received a free airline ticket. I never expected to use it since work kept me so busy and the problems with Delight made travel difficult. But since the ticket caught my eye I pulled it off the board and took a closer look. It was due to expire in just a few days. It seemed as if the Lord was saying "Go. I've made a way for you." So I went.

The conference was like nothing I had ever experienced before. It was so freeing to be in an atmosphere of love and acceptance among people with stories similar to my own. Celebrate Recovery is a place where your identity rests firmly in Christ, and though you name your struggles, you are not defined by them. The Lord really touched my heart there, and as I listened to testimonies of others like me, I realized that my testimony could encourage many people as well. I began to believe that the Lord could use what I had considered shameful to bring honor to Him and encouragement to others.

The twelfth step in Celebrate Recovery's program says, "Having had a spiritual experience as a result of these steps, we try to carry this message to others and to practice these principles in all our affairs." It wasn't long before the Lord began opening up doors for me to begin doing just that. Not long after the conference in California I helped to start a Celebrate Recovery at Cedar Ridge. It wasn't long however, before Craig, my first Celebrate Recovery leader, asked me to come to Church of the Redeemer and begin a men's group at the local jail. Ever since my experience in jail, I had a burden to help the incarcerated. So I accepted. Delight became a member of Church of the Redeemer and began serving in their Celebrate Recovery program. We quickly got accustomed to being in a larger church and enjoyed the teachings of Pastor Dale, the senior pastor there. We had found another church home.

One of the things I learned in recovery was that it takes more than just showing up to meetings to get the healing. You have to do the work. In Celebrate Recovery that means having accountability partners, sharing honestly in group, coming regularly, and really trying to apply the lessons to your life. Delight attended once or twice or month and wanted to become a leader too. Leaders facilitated the sharing groups and strove to make their lives as trans-parent as possible in hopes of encouraging others. Delight knew what she wanted, but she didn't want to commit to the work and personal change required. Although her addictions were not out of control at this time, she was still in denial about how deep her dysfunction and issues were. I had discovered that when we don't face the things in our past, and uncover how they control our thoughts, actions, and reactions today, we can't be free to serve the Lord.

In 2003, I was still eagerly serving the Lord at Celebrate Recovery. But I wanted more. I wanted the Lord to use me in a bigger way and really make a difference for Him. As I prayed, the Lord said, *"Listen to the Holy Spirit, you'll go down and help someone in Washington, D.C. You'll also go back to Georgia and start Celebrate Recovery with Bill Smith in the jail and community there."*

At the time I didn't know who in D.C. the Lord was talking about. Then our friend Carmen, a talented singer and songwriter, told me there was a lady doing ministry in downtown D.C. that I should meet. So one evening while Delight was in bed, I went downtown and met the Chief of Police and Carmen's contact, Reverend Talbert. Reverend Talbert had been doing prison ministry for about twenty years. Her church was not a wealthy one, so she relied on grants and government support. She had a mentoring program which placed her in the thick of crime and street fights. I wasn't sure what she saw in me, but Reverend Talbert wanted me to come alongside her and join in the work. I mentored several inmates and started a Celebrate Recovery group for re-entry men recently released from jail. After I'd been working with her ministry for awhile, she sent me to a meeting at the Capitol, and I met Chuck Colson, founder of Prison Fellowship Ministries. It was part of a legislative signing event for a bill being passed to protect inmates from sexual attacks.

It wasn't long before I knew it was time to go to Georgia. The Holy Spirit kept drawing my heart back to the place where it all began for me. I took Delight with me. She was still on medication, but she was trying to get off of it, so we went. It was God's timing. I'd told the sheriff that I wanted to start Celebrate Recovery there, and he set up meetings with six different pastors to help get things going. Tim Rice, one of the pastors I met with, had a congregant that had just overdosed, and the idea of bringing Celebrate Recovery to his church sounded like God's perfect timing. It felt like we'd been brought there just for him.

We stayed for about a week in Georgia, meeting with the different pastors, encouraging them to start Celebrate

Recovery. Tim led the charge with the other pastors and by the end of the week all six pastors had made a commitment to start the program. Delight and I had to return home to keep our business running, but every few months we went down to check on their progress. After Celebrate Recovery got going in the community, we introduced it to the jail where I'd been arrested, and the program flourished there as well. During those first few months I wondered how everything would keep going without me there to help oversee things. The Holy Spirit took care of it all for me. Everyone was on fire to either get free from bondage or help others do so, and the ministry just expanded and blossomed on its own. I continued to visit for several years, but God was the one making it happen.

It seemed as if I was riding a spiritual wave! I was amazed at how God was using me, a former drug dealer and addict. The Lord had allowed my testimony to encourage others in Georgia and even around the nation. *Inside Journal*, Prison Fellowship's newspaper for prisoners, did a story on me, and I began to learn more about what that organization did for men and women in jail. I began to see how what I had learned in Celebrate Recovery could be a great addition to the work of Prison Fellowship. It had the potential to help the men in jail get free from their past and be able to start a new life that was free from the bondages that so many of them slipped back into after being released.

Delight and I worked tirelessly to connect Chuck Colson of Prison Fellowship and Rick Warren and Jon Baker of Celebrate Recovery. We made presentation folders about Celebrate Recovery and even made a videotape of the Celebrate Recovery conference to share with Prison Fellowship. Delight spoke with people both at Prison Fellowship and Celebrate Recovery numerous times to try to set up a meeting and share one another's visions. We were sure that once both groups got to know each other, they would see how a partnership could help a lot of people. Eventually the two groups did begin communicating and today CR Inside is the jail ministry of Celebrate Recovery. The partnership with Prison Fellowship allowed Celebrate Recovery to move into prisons all across the United States much more quickly than if they had started out on their own.

Meeting Chuck Colson in Washington, D.C.

These two years of working with Celebrate Recovery and Prison Fellowship were an exciting time for both Delight and me. Delight was so excited about working with everyone. She committed to stop taking her medications and trying to clean up. Our mission grew clear. We would open recovery houses for those transitioning from prison back to life on the outside. The need was great, and the Lord placed a burning desire in my heart to see this happen, not only in Maryland, but all over the country. Delight, being the loyal and supportive woman that she'd always been, was behind me 100 percent. She was so giving and loving, always wanting to help other people. I still had faith that the Lord would somehow reach Delight and bring her a complete and full healing. I looked forward to the day that we could serve the Lord together without all the baggage of our past hindering our relationship with each other and with the Lord.

As I got more involved in this work, my life was turned over yet again. Delight was excited too, but she still wasn't willing to relinquish her addictions. Delight started going to Georgetown Pain Clinic, but to my surprise and dismay, the professionals there only prescribed her a different kind of pain medication—methadone. The methadone made her throw up. She couldn't eat and the drinking continued. Carmen, the woman who introduced us to Reverend Talbert in D.C, would occasionally come over and try to get her to walk around the house and eat and make sure she wasn't drinking.

Over the next three years, the nightmare of addiction took over our lives again. By manipulating different doctors to get the prescription she wanted, Delight once again became utterly addicted to OxyContin. This drug, in addition to her increased drinking, migraine medications, and sleeping pills, changed my wife and brought out all of her demons. At times her body would go into convulsions, and I felt so helpless. Whenever I left the house I was worried to death she would have an episode and I wouldn't be there to help her. There were three or four times I found her unconscious in the house and had to rush her to the emergency room, not knowing if she would live or die. One time she fell, caught her foot under a kitchen cabinet, and broke her ankle. My own co-dependency kept me from realizing the dire situation she was in. I knew things weren't right, but I didn't really understand the depths of her growing addiction. I kept asking her if she was drinking, but she always said that she wasn't. I wanted to believe the best and this kept me in denial about what was really going on.

I was so desperate for answers that I decided to videotape her when she was unconscious. I used the tape to try to convince the doctors that Delight needed more help than just pain medication. We finally got her to see a doctor in Baltimore to try and find out what was wrong with her. After they analyzed her, they told her that her system was overwhelmed with pain medications. She didn't want to hear it. By moving among several doctors, she was able to continue her steady supply of OxyContin. I tried to talk with the doctors about her growing addiction, but they didn't want to talk with me. Delight refused to allow me to go with her to her appointments and had directed her doctors not to speak with me.

Finally, I proposed the idea of her going to a Christian rehab center in Arizona. Everything had just gotten so out of hand, and I didn't know what else to do. She consented to go to the center in Arizona, but she hated me for it. I flew out there with her for support and she stayed for a week, but then decided she wanted to come back and do it her way. Delight wanted to get rid of her pain and addictions, but she wouldn't go through the *entire* process necessary for freedom. She would go so far but then pull back.

Delight's bondage to her addictions was a vicious cycle that had steadily increased in intensity throughout our marriage. I had sought help from medical doctors, Christian therapists, recovery groups, and rehabilitation programs. None seemed to be able to break through to Delight. I knew that her bondage was rooted in a spiritual battle with Satan. In the Bible in Ephesians 6:12, it says "For our struggle is not against flesh and blood, but against the rulers, against the authorities, against the powers of this dark world and against the spiritual forces of evil in the heavenly realms." As I watched my wife fight her battle, I knew that I didn't understand the spiritual battle. I certainly didn't feel equipped to fight it, but I was determined to learn. So I began a journey of my own to go deeper into God's truth and seek His guidance for me, for Delight, and ultimately His will for my life. I was not disappointed in my search. What unfolded over the next few months became what I call my first revelation. It all began with a visit to the doctor's office.

Delight and I had started seeing a Christian doctor in Florida, Dr. Don Colbert. Although it was a long way from Maryland, he was the only doctor I knew of that might be able to help Delight. He uses an integrative approach to medicine, employing natural, holistic remedies as well as traditional medical approaches. He also emphasizes the spiritual side of health and is a strong proponent of prayer and fasting as part of a healthy lifestyle. In 2006, during one of our visits to see Dr. Colbert, he recommended a book for me to read, *The Bondage Breaker* by Neil Anderson. This book opened my eyes to the reality of spiritual warfare and I began to understand even more deeply how Satan works in our lives to keep us from the freedom and grace promised by God.

Several years earlier, I had received the gift of the Holy Spirit while on a men's retreat. I wanted any and every tool that was available to combat Satan, so I eagerly stood up to be prayed over. At the time I knew I had taken an important step in my growth, but now I felt as if there was so much more for me to learn and to experience.

Reading the book whetted my appetite to learn more about the spiritual realm. I especially wanted to know about spiritual gifts. I had heard many times that Christians had been given gifts to be used in ministry. I was looking for my gift. How would I know if I had one? How did I find out what it was? How would I learn how to use it and make it grow? Pastor Dale encouraged the congregation to desire all that God had to offer us. I desperately wanted it all—but didn't know how to get it or even what it might look like in reality!

I wasn't learning what I needed from church sermons,

and not knowing what else to do, I shared with my friend Carmen what I was struggling with. She recommended another book for me to read, *Pigs in the Parlor* by Frank Hammond. This book really began to put it all in perspective for me. I still remember the day it all clicked for me. I was driving down the road thinking about what the book had to say about the spiritual battle we are all a part of. Suddenly it was like my life flashed before my eyes and every event that had happened to me took on new significance. I finally understood what my life had been about and why certain things had happened to me. This was my revelation; it was a new and deeper understanding about my life. Tears streamed down my face as I was filled with joy. I saw how the Lord had brought me through all of those battles. From my sexual abuse as a boy to my days at the mental hospital to the insane thinking that caused my car accidents to the chaos of my drug running to my involvement with Doc and his cult. It all finally made sense. I was so excited about this understanding that I pulled over on the side of the road and began calling Carmen and another friend who were my spiritual support team. I had to share with them what I now understood about my life.

In recovery, I knew we couldn't simply address the mind and body; we also had to address what was going on spiritually with a person as well. I felt a tremendous surge of spiritual growth. This was what I had been waiting for. From all I had learned about spiritual gifts, it seemed that I was given the gift of spiritual discernment to understand and "see" the spiritual reality of the world around me. I'd always been aware of the spiritual realm, even before I understood what it was and what it was about. It was apparent to me now that there was a constant spiritual battle raging all around us. And, the Lord made it clear to me that delivering people from demonic bondage was part of what I should be doing with my ministry.

About two weeks after this new understanding, I was

still riding a wave of spiritual energy and excitement when I got a chance to put into practice what I had been learning. Pastor Dale from Church of the Redeemer came to Celebrate Recovery to preach. In seven years of being involved in Celebrate Recovery, this was the first time I had heard him preach there. It was sure to be a special night. The message centered on the passage in the Gospels when Christ's disciples hadn't been able to cast out demons on their own. There was a man in my group who had tried to commit suicide several times, and I felt the desire to cast that demon out. At the end of the sermon I tried to get to Pastor Dale for support, but it felt like an obstacle course. A wall of people kept me from reaching him. I tried to get to Craig, the Celebrate Recovery Director, but again was blocked by the crowd. I realized that I had to do this myself and not rely on anyone else. So, I asked the gentlemen if I could pray for him myself. I laid hands on him to cast the suicidal demon out, believing in faith that my attempt at spiritual warfare was successful. The next day as I was journaling, I realized the day that I'd prayed for him was June 6, 2006 – 666. It was like a confirmation that the Lord wanted me to persevere, and I was on the right path. I believed that I could use my new understanding to help people, especially my wife. I was still convinced that Delight could be healed by me or someone else. I wondered if this new insight and gift of spiritual discernment was the Lord's way of giving me the right tools to reach Delight. In my eagerness to see Delight find the freedom and healing that I knew, I still didn't understand the importance of *her* role in her healing. *She* had to be willing to surrender to the Lord.

I had another experience with the spiritual realm not long after this first one. One of the members of my Celebrate Recovery group had a traumatic childhood experience and seemed to be struggling with it quite a bit. I decided to go and see him, hoping to pray against the spirits that seemed to be attacking his life. When he came to the door to let me in, I didn't recognize him. It was as if he had a different face. As we walked through the house, it seemed as if his face gradually returned to normal. I was so shocked, I was only able to pray briefly for him and then left. Later, I returned to pray for him again, but this time I went with another Christian who was more experienced in spiritual warfare. Through this experience I was convinced that I had been given yet another glimpse of the spiritual realm that surrounds us.

I was excited about my experiences but knew I had much to learn. I went to Pastor Dale to share with him what I had experienced and to learn what I could from him. He advised me to take it slowly, read some books and really get acquainted with the process. It wasn't the answer I was looking for, as I felt ready to plunge into this new ministry and I was hoping for a mentor to teach me what I needed to know. I talked about it with Carmen, her husband, and my sister Pam, and they too advised me to be careful. They were afraid that I would come under spiritual attack before I was ready. They convinced me to slow down, although I had no doubt in my mind that this is what the Lord was calling me to pursue. I agreed to slow down and knew that I had a lot to learn. I prayed that this would be an area of ministry for me in the future.

The advice to slow things down was certainly from God. He knew what was coming ahead for me and Delight. My revelation was a spiritual high that I would rely on to get me through the next few years. Satan's attacks on me were vicious. The next three years, 2006 through early 2009, were some of the most intense and challenging years of my life. During this time I was in danger of losing both my business and my home. Delight's bondage became even more severe. I would face the loss of my mother, my brother-in-law Walter, and ultimately my wife.

Financially, Delight and I were struggling. We were heavily in debt after building our latest house and carried a mortgage of nearly $8,000 a month for both our business and our home. In order for Craftmasters to grow as a company, we needed to expand our work into Washington, D.C. Delight was hugely instrumental in getting a business license to operate in D.C. This opened the door for receiving our biggest contract ever for $4 million to install flooring for an entire city block under construction. The only hitch was that we needed to have a business address in D.C., and taking on a monthly rental seemed impossible. I was installing carpet in an office building in Georgetown, a high-priced, classy neighborhood in D.C. I asked the owner what he would charge for renting an office space there. His response was, "Don't worry about it. Just install the carpet, and we'll call it even." That was in 2006 and we still have not had to pay rent to him for the office space. Once again, God came through and seemed to be saying that it was okay for us to go ahead with the huge contract we had just been awarded. Although this would stretch our little company more than ever, it seemed like the opportunity for us to move to the next level.

Managing the large contract, we had received in D.C. meant running three large jobs at the same time. I had forty subcontractors working for me and tight deadlines to meet. The normal obstacles of any job had multiplied due to the size of this one. I had to use our home as collateral for a bond to insure the job. If we didn't finish on time we could lose our home. The pressure was intense.

I decided to partner with another company, owned by Christians, to help complete the job. I was afraid Craftmasters might have taken on more than it could handle. With so much on the line, I couldn't take a chance of failing. We agreed to give them a percent of the profits once the job was finished.

The entire job took about three years to complete and at the end of the job, as we prepared to complete the last three floors, the entire project nearly came undone. It was the most difficult time of my life and the hardest test the Lord has ever put me through.

The company I had partnered with was afraid that they wouldn't receive their money and demanded that I pay them their share before the job was finished. I couldn't do that because I hadn't been paid yet. Since they were warehousing the materials I needed to complete the final four floors of the last building, they refused to release the materials until I had paid them. I pleaded on the phone with them to allow me to finish the job first. But they refused. I managed to come up with $80,000 to pay them by asking for early payment from the construction company managing the job. I finally received most of the materials I needed. I was still short material, however, to finish the final floor. I was deeply hurt that my Christian brothers had no compassion to extend to me. I was strongly tempted by Satan to use these same tactics against them. After going on a retreat with the other Celebrate Recovery leaders at my church and praying with the Christian men around me, I decided to walk away from the situation and not pursue legal action against them. At the same time that this was happening, the construction company that managed the project was threatening to kick me off the job, if I didn't fix a problem with the final floor we were working on. The problem was a major repair and was not in my contract to fix. The company didn't want to hear it. They knew I needed this job and thought they could strong arm me into doing the extra work that had not been included in the contract.

I prayed harder than ever and the Lord proved His faithfulness. A flooring supplier agreed to front me the material I needed to finish the job, accepting payment later, despite the fact that I already owed them $120,000. Then ten of the construction company project managers and foremen met with me to force me to correct the flooring problem. I prayed as I went in, prepared for the worst. But not one of them could make a case that I was responsible for the repair. They agreed to hire another company to do the work that was not part of my contract.

By the time this job was completed, I was hoping to, at most, break even. I had learned a lot from the experiences, even if I hadn't made much money on it. After all of the trouble and hardship, the owner of the construction company would only pay me a part of my full contract. With bills of my own to pay I couldn't risk destroying my relationship with my own suppliers and putting my whole business at risk. A lawsuit was out of the question, it would be too costly and take too long. After settling for $.70 for each dollar owed to me, we made about $110,000 profit on the job that took three years. Although our house mortgage was still high, our business debts were paid. We were making progress.

Chapter 13

A New Covenant

The incredible stress and challenge during that three year construction job had taken a toll on my health, especially the last year as I tried to finish the job. I suffered from chronic intestinal pain and discomfort, and my stress levels had never been higher. At the same time that I was faced with the challenges of the job, I continued to face the challenges of living with Delight's addictions. Her addictions and depression caused her to stumble around the house, unaware of her surroundings. I was terrified that she would fall and injure herself. She was worse than I had ever seen her. Things were escalating out of control.

After completing the job, our intention was to sell our house, get out of debt, and rebuild the house I grew up in that we had been renting out for several years. One day in late spring 2007, we were at a stone quarry to pick stone for the new house we were building and Delight slipped and fell, pulling her shoulder out of its socket. As a result she got another prescription for OxyContin, as well as another prescription for sleeping medication because she was having a hard time sleeping. On top of all of this, she was also taking pills for headaches. I tried to talk to her doctors about all the drugs she was getting, but because of the privacy form that prohibited the doctors from discussing her condition or prescriptions with me. I couldn't intervene. We were once again stuck in this hellish cycle.

When I found a straw, I knew she'd started crushing up the OxyContin and snorting it. I didn't know what else to do, so I called her friends, including Mary Kay and Carmen, and we had an intervention. This was serious, and I wanted to try and find some way to break Delight out of denial. Unfortunately, the intervention didn't work. Instead of accepting that her life was out of control, she responded by lashing out defensively at everyone in the room. All I could do was sit back and cry. Finally, I gave her a choice. She could go to a rehab center or follow Dr. Colbert's advice and attend a deliverance ministry. But, Delight still believed she could do it on her own and refused to go to either.

At first, as was typical, she made some positive steps, but soon went back to using again. The migraines started to come back. Then came the drinking and sleeping pills. Her depression was so bad that four or five days would go by and she wouldn't even leave our bedroom. The hellish cycle began again.

In the midst of all of this there was a bright spot, a memory I will cherish forever. I got to watch my mother grow closer to the Lord. I asked her for forgiveness and told her how sorry I was for everything that I put the family through. We made beautiful amends and our relationship got better and better. Christ's love was a beautiful healer. Before she died, she'd started praying. And, on Mother's Day, Delight and I took her to Faith Tabernacle down in D.C. It was amazing that she wanted to go out with us at all, as she didn't attend church and preferred to keep to her routines. She spent that day in an African American Pentecostal church where there was loud praying and people jumping in worship. It was totally different from her Catholic upbringing, but she loved it. The Lord also blessed us with a special dinner together that night. When we got to the restaurant, we found that it wouldn't open for another hour. But amazingly, they let us in anyway, and told us we could sit down at a table. We had a wonderful time just talking and being together. This was our last chance to spend time with her. My mother died that night.

A week before she died, she'd given me a picture of her holding me. I'd never seen that picture before. In that picture I could see that she had done her best to care for and watch over me. With the loss of my mother, the financial stress, and Delight's struggles, I needed the Lord more than ever. I didn't know it, but the Lord was preparing to give me a second revelation about his plans for my life. This encounter with the Lord would set my life firmly on a path of hope, rather than despair and discouragement.

It was now 2008 and the Lakelands Revival was in full swing. My sister Pam had encouraged me to watch it on God TV and see if it might be something that would help Delight if she were to watch it as well. After the experience of the intervention, I was more convinced than ever that Delight was caught in a spiritual battle and needed a spiritual deliverance for her physical addictions. I began watching and listening to Todd Bentley preach and heal. As I watched people being delivered at the revival, I couldn't help but wonder what happened to them later. Did they stay delivered? Was it a struggle? How did they not fall prey to spiritual attack again? I knew that a one-time deliverance was only a first step; there was much more that needed to happen for a person to be truly free. I really wanted to learn and understand about spiritual deliverance and healing. Because of my dyslexia, I have a hard time reading the Bible and gaining insights from my reading. The Lord usually speaks to me through prayer and other people. When I asked God, "What does this all mean?" I received a strong word from the Lord telling me to read Hebrews. So I did. Reading Hebrews 2:1-4, it was as if the scripture came alive in front of my eyes. It was a warning to pay attention. "God also testified to it by signs, wonders and various miracles, and gifts of the Holy Spirit distributed according to his will."

I wanted a sign from God to let me know that I'd heard Him correctly, something that was confirmation of the wonders occurring in my spirit. One Saturday, I was working on a house we were building right next to the house where we lived. I loved that property. I'd spent my entire life there. It was the first place that I had an encounter with the spiritual realm, seeing that angel in the treetops when I was a young boy. As I worked outside that day, I thought I felt someone behind me. I jumped and turned to see who it was, but no one was there—I thought I saw a fleeting figure in black pants, but I let it go. A few hours later, it started to rain. When the sun came back out, I said to Delight, "There should be a rainbow." As I said this, Delight looked out the window and saw a beautiful rainbow, right in our yard about twenty feet away. It was like a special gift, a sign and wonder, a promise from God that He would show us His glory. I learned later that the rainbow is the sign of a covenant between the Lord and his people. I had a covenant with the Lord.

A rainbow appeared in the backyard of our 1115 home. I took it as a covenant rainbow for God's promises to me. This weekend changed my life.

That evening I knew that a pastor from Lakelands who worked with Todd Bentley was at Immanuel's Church, just one mile from our house. I hoped that Delight might receive a touch from the Lord at the service. While we were there, I was sitting praying for Delight, when someone in the back caught my eye. He was wearing black pants, and as our eyes met, I felt we had a connection, so somehow I expected him to talk to me. Sure enough, during the service, the man came up to me and told me he had a word from the Lord.

"The Lord has chosen you. You will feed many. The Lord will bless your walk. Do not worry. He has you covered." I was amazed, no one had ever prophesied over me before. I felt as though God Himself was speaking out of this man's mouth.

That night I had two dreams. In one dream I was on a boat. Craig Brown, my friend and the director of Celebrate Recovery at my church, was in the boat. I wanted to try to walk on water, but I fell under the waves and drowned. But I didn't stay dead; I was brought back to life. In the second dream there was a man dressed in a red tuxedo, and he had a gun. He shot me, but the bullets couldn't harm me. The Lord was telling me that death and Satan no longer had any power over me.

I would never be the same after that day. I was so glad the Lord gave me ears to hear, eyes to see and a mind to receive His message for me. I wanted to tap into the power of the Lord. A baptism of the supernatural was on its way, and I was ready. I would walk with Him as fast as He could take me. There were so many overwhelming and beautiful thoughts swirling in my mind because of the Lord. I was high on the Holy Spirit. I talked with two Christian brothers and told them of my revelation. I was filled with the Holy Spirit and the words just ran out of my mouth. It was almost like there was heavenly dust floating around me as I spoke freely with them. It was amazing.

One of the men I spoke to was Craig. I shared how the Lord was making it clear to me that I was being equipped and given the task of bringing the message of recovery to more people. I wanted to open a recovery center where men and women could find the peace and freedom from their hurts, habits, and hang-ups just as I had. I was sure the

Lord was saying it was time to start making that happen. I told Craig that I believed he was a part of this big picture too. Somehow he and I would work together to make this happen. As I spoke to him, I felt myself shaking, full of the Holy Spirit. I had never spoken to anyone like that before but, I felt a new confidence and boldness as a result of the dreams and prophecies I had experienced.

Others started to sprinkle doubt into what I'd heard from the man who spoke to me in the church service. They said things like, "He could be a crazy man. Does anyone even know who it was?" So, I decided to seek him out and find him again. I found out that he had a "Prayer Stop" on New Hampshire Avenue. The Prayer Stop, located next to Immanuel's Church (which is where we first met), is a very small air conditioned furnished shed where this man prays with whoever stops there. I learned that his name was Dennis.

He told me that because the message was from the Lord to *me*, that he couldn't remember it. It was between God and me. But he prayed over me again, and this was the new message: "The Lord will take you out of debt. You will be debt free. All your bills will be paid. You'll have a baby. The Lord will put you in a new place." This seemed an impossible prophecy to me. I certainly couldn't see how it might happen. Delight and I were so deeply in debt we were at risk of losing our home, we had no major work contracts lined up, and Delight was unable to have children. Then Dennis told me to make sure I went to Immanuel's Church the following weekend because a guest speaker would be there that I needed to hear.

I went home that day and when I checked the mail, a contract for a million and a half dollar job was there. It was an overwhelming confirmation of my covenant with the Lord. God was keeping his hands faithfully on me, and I didn't have to wonder how He would fulfill the promise of those other words that were spoken to me that day. He'd always kept His promises, and I could believe in nothing less.

I was looking forward to hearing the guest speaker the following weekend. The Lord seemed to be leading me in a new direction, I just wasn't sure where. I knew, though, that if I was obedient to what the Lord was showing me, He would take care of the details. When I went to Immanuel's Church the next weekend to hear the guest speaker, I heard the Senior Pastor of Hope Christian Church, Bishop Harry Jackson. He talked about a new wineskin, about the Lord pouring new wine into people who were willing to be filled with His Spirit and do new things. I knew this message was meant for me to hear, and my excitement at God's presence in my life only grew. I managed to speak to the Bishop for a moment as he left the church that evening and he prayed for me. Throughout the next several weeks it seemed as if I heard the Bishop each time I turned on the radio or TV. God seemed to be confirming that I was to listen to this man. Within a week I was sitting in the Bishop's office sharing with him my dream of opening a recovery center in the area. I also shared how I wanted to use my testimony to give people hope that nothing is impossible with God. For the past several years I had recorded my story, sending the tapes to a ghost writer to be transcribed. My dream included using the book to share my vision. I was amazed that this man who I had just met was already so willing to listen to me and encourage me to pursue my dreams.

Bishop Jackson's church was only fifteen minutes from my house. I decided to visit the church and hear one of his sermons. When I entered the church, I noticed a friend I hadn't seen in fifteen years. He saw me and quickly motioned for me to join him in the front row. I immediately felt comfortable and knew this was no coincidence. It was one of God's divine appointments.

Feeling empowered that the Lord was with me and was using signs, wonders, and miracles, I convinced Delight to drive down to Florida to visit the Lakeland Revival and have Todd Bentley pray over her. But we never got there. On the drive down, Delight was so out of it that she got out of the car at a red-light and headed into oncoming traffic. A car swerved and just missed her. I decided to take her to Dr. Colbert's office in Orlando instead. He was one of the few doctors we had met with that believed Delight could be healed without the use of prescription medications. He also fully understood the spiritual battle of addiction and would be able to give us godly advice. When we got to his office, Delight could not stand on her own two feet. Dr. Colbert gave her an IV to revive her. After talking together, he advised her once again to go to the John Hagee deliverance meetings in Texas. We'd tried most everything else, so we figured, why not?

Like most addicts, life is a series of steep ups and even steeper downs. After Dr. Colbert she was on an upswing and I wanted to take advantage of it. So a few weeks later, Delight went out by herself to Texas. Before she left, I had put it on the line for her. If she didn't go I was going to have to move out. I had no intention of divorcing her, but I could no longer try to support her and help her through her addictions. She had to decide to change on her own. All of my hoping, helping, and rescuing hadn't worked. It was up to her to decide the pain of recovery was worth the price of healing.

The deliverance meetings included three days of workshops and a final deliverance meeting at the end. When Delight returned home, I could see a difference immediately. Her eyes looked so bright and she talked about getting back on her feet. The next night after returning home she relapsed. I later learned she hadn't attended the entire meeting. She'd left at the end before they did the final deliverance. You can chase the spirit out of you, Jesus warned us, but if you don't put the right stuff back in it'll bring back seven more spirits.(Luke 11:24-26) Despite this disappointment, Delight was willing to see Dr. Kim again. She knew she needed help and was at least reaching out for it. I wasn't going to move out as long as she was trying to get help.

It was now October of 2008. It had been quite a year of drama and crisis, but it wasn't over yet. My sister Pam and her husband, Walter, had been tremendous supports for me throughout my life. Over the previous year, Walter worked for me at Craftmasters, helping to finish out a big job that had ended two weeks earlier. We had grown close over that time, gaining a new respect for each other. He and my sister had been high school sweethearts and still did everything together, including teaching tennis classes. One afternoon in October, Walter tripped as he ran backwards to reach a ball hit. He lost his footing and fell hard, hitting his head on the pavement. He never regained consciousness and died the next day. It was a painful and unexpected blow to our family, leaving all of us shocked and shaken.

Pam has always been the bedrock of our family. She and Walter had stood by me and Delight, seeing us through our many crises. Since they lived on the same street as us, they had seen into our lives more than most. Walter's death was certainly a challenge to our faith. Why would God allow this to happen? It was Pam's trust in God—that he had a reason and that it didn't change his love for us—that helped all of us through this time.

As the year began to draw to a close, I decided to go on a twenty-one day fast. A lot had happened in the last year that had shaken up my world and my relationship with the Lord. I hoped to focus in on what the Lord seemed to be telling me about the future, find peace and confidence in Him in the midst of all of my struggles, and hopefully experience some breakthroughs in my own life to take into the upcoming year. Delight seemed to be doing better, although she spent most of her time in bed still. Her thoughts were clearer and more focused. It was during the first few days of the fast that I received an ad in the mail for a cruise.

Chapter 14

Experiencing Love

For at least the last six months of my wife Delight's life, I would wake up at night and pray over her, fighting the spiritual battle that needed to be fought, standing in the gap for her. The demons of her family history were plaguing her. She told me that she'd been drinking and hiding it. Just as her mother had been before her, she was also addicted to pain medication. And then there was the matter of sexual abuse by her brothers that she'd never really healed from since childhood. The last two years of her life had been difficult ones to deal with. Her wounds were festering, and she'd been trying the wrong bandages for so long now. There were times when I could see the light in her eyes and other times, when I couldn't even believe she was the person I knew and loved. Addictions have such power to change your personality.

Throughout Delight's addiction, I struggled with how to best love and support my wife. There were times when I had to carry her to bed, times when she verbally abused me, and then, times when she begged for help promising to change her ways. Sometimes I struggled on this roller coaster, but I could rest assured, that I'd pleased the Lord by turning my life around to be a servant to her. I had learned this difficult truth from a marriage class I took at my church, Church of the Redeemer. Through this class the Holy Spirit touched me and opened my eyes to what it meant to be a servant to my wife. A servant's heart is the foundation of marriage. This covenant understanding is such a beautiful way to treat a spouse. I'd finally under-stood what the Lord wanted out of our marriage. I never would have learned this if I hadn't been willing to seek out support and encouragement on my own. I attended the marriage class by myself, not waiting for Delight to attend with me. I took the class twice because I knew I really needed to change and grow in my marriage. I had a support team of other men whom I called when I needed encouragement. Regardless of what was going on with my wife, I needed to please God with how I treated the gift He gave me.

At the same time that Delight was struggling, I had been under a tremendous attack from a business agreement that had gone bad. This season had been the toughest time in my life. It was crushing me. The business situation had put me at risk for losing my house as well as my business. Delight's choices were putting me at risk of losing my wife. I was truly in a desperate situation. Thanks to my support team at church and my best friend, Christ, I was able to stay strong through it all.

Since all I wanted was for her to have a breakthrough, I decided to go on a twenty-one day fast (my longest yet) to petition for her before the Lord. It was during this 21 day fast that the Lord really spoke to me about living life His way.

Fasting has remained a way for me to get in touch with the Lord. I started the practice, as a spiritual discipline, while I was incarcerated and prayed that God would give me an early release. Fasting is a way for me to let go of my flesh and focus on the Spirit. It keeps the door of my heart open to God. It allows me to hear Him more clearly. It also helps me in the spiritual battles I continue to face in this life. Not only does fasting help cleanse the spirit, it also cleanses toxins from the body. During this extended fast I wanted to make sure that I was taking care of my spiritual and physical health. So, using Dr. Colbert's book, *Fasting Made Easy*, as a tool, I started my fast the night of November 27th, 2008.

There had been a lot of turmoil in Delight and my relationship. I really wanted to help her feel better. We had recently met with our bishop, and she was unexpectedly open with him about her drinking and her need for help. I was hopeful that things were headed in the right direction.

Things seemed to be improving. Delight was being more open about her need for help. So, we decided to go on a cruise for my birthday. The Lord said to me, "Go away and spend time together. You've worked hard. Enjoy yourselves." I was really looking forward to the cruise, still praying Delight would turn things around. God was right. We *had* been working hard, developing and maintaining our own business. When you own your business and work out of your home, sometimes it feels like work is all-encompassing. Planning this cruise felt like planning for a honeymoon.

Before we left, the Lord pushed me to get a will done. We had tried for over ten years to write a will, but something always kept us from finishing the process. For some reason I couldn't get it off my mind that we needed to finish the will. I felt a sense of urgency about it that I couldn't explain. Finally, a few days before we left, I got it done.

The night before we left, Pastor Joey and his wife Missy came over. Pastor Joey led the marriage class that we'd been attending at our church. The visit with Joey and Missy turned into a beautiful time of fellowship and prayer. And, as we prayed, we anointed Delight with oil. Afterward, Delight said she really felt something, that she was touched and moved by the Holy Spirit. Everything seemed to be going so well; something special was going on.

On past trips, we usually over-packed, rushed out of the house to make it to the airport on time, and felt generally stressed by the travel. This time it was different. We didn't over-pack, and Delight didn't even take any jewelry with her. She promised to pack some medication that had been prescribed by her psychiatrist, which she had refused to take thus far. I hoped that if she took the medication it would help her get back on track. We left for the airport on time and had a smooth trip to Ft.

168 – Against All Odds

Lauderdale, where the cruise ship was docked. Beforehand, I'd tried to book us an ocean-view room in our hotel, however it turned out to be too expensive. But once we arrived at check-in, we got an ocean-view room on the thirteenth floor given to us for no extra charge. We weren't sailing for two days, so we had some time in Ft. Lauderdale to ourselves. Our first day was my birthday and when we went to dinner, we had the best dinner we ever had in our life. The food, the service—everything was incredible. Our second night we decided to go back to the same restaurant and once again had another beautiful dinner. It was like the Father's hand was right there, blessing us with a beautiful vacation.

After our second evening in Ft. Lauderdale, Delight began to feel poorly. For the past fifteen years, she'd struggled with headaches that got so bad they'd make her vomit. She lost weight because she couldn't keep anything down. We'd gone to the hospital multiple times in the last year, where the doctors gave her something to try and keep her from vomiting. I worried that if she didn't get better, she might need medical attention.

We got on the boat on Sunday and Delight still didn't feel well. What I didn't know then was that she'd brought along OxyContin, a prescription painkiller that has nasty side effects if not taken in the correct dosages. According to the DEA, abusing the drug can cause "severe respiratory depression, skeletal muscle flaccidity, cold and clammy skin, reduction in blood pressure and heart rate, coma, respiratory arrest, and death."[1] I knew that a lot of her symptoms over the past few years had been related to her misuse of OxyContin. Part of the reason why it's so dangerous is because, in Delight's case, doctors kept prescribing it to her, and the more she obtained, the more she wanted. It was an easy drug to abuse and become dependent upon. Yet, none of her doctors were stopping

---

[1] United States Department of Justice. *Justice.gov.* n.d.
www.justice.gov/dea/concern/oxycontin.html

her from taking it. Delight also brought along some other medicine but I caught her with it so she asked me to help hold her accountable. I gave her a half a pill a day so that she could try and come off of it slowly.

On Monday we were at sea all day, and she was throwing up so much she couldn't eat. Tuesday was the same. Because of all of our past struggles, we were not normally very affectionate with one another. But that day, I got into bed with her and held her. I'm so glad I did that now since it was one of our last moments together. We watched a movie, and then I asked her to go to the sick bay on the ship. She didn't want to go.

Seven o'clock rolled around and I'd made dinner reservations for both of us in hopes that she would've felt better by then. But in one glance, it was easy to see that she was still sick. I took her down to the sick bay where they gave her an IV and told me they were going to take care of her. Back in our room, I took a quick shower, and went back to check on her. She was throwing up again, and they said they were going to give her some medicine to help her stop throwing up. I thought that this would be the same process that we typically went through at the hospital, so I went on ahead to dinner. Oddly enough, I was thinking of Paul McCartney and the death of his wife, Linda. What would it be like to have your spouse—lover, friend, long-time partner—die? I was so restless at dinner that I got up after my appetizer. I had to check on her again. I went to talk to the guy at the front desk. He said she'd stopped throwing up, but she still had a migraine, and they were going to give her some pain medication. Reluctantly, I went back to the restaurant to finish my meal, thinking that it would take about an hour before her medication kicked in and she started to feel better. When I came back, the doctors told me that Delight had died.

What? Shock and grief filled me. It seemed like everyone started asking me questions at once. *Do you want a tranquilizer?* No. As painful as it was, I wanted to feel it all, be alert, and understand what was happening. *Can I ask you some questions about your wife's prior health?* No. I just wanted to be by myself.

They let me be alone with her, and I gently took her wedding ring and necklace off. I prayed for the Lord to resurrect her, to bring her back, just in case He was waiting for me to pray that prayer. I wish I could've done it more strongly, but I accepted that it was His will for me to let her go. I held her hand and touched her hair, kissed her mouth, and then her eyes. I just sat there and rubbed her hair. I felt a freedom for her. I was grateful for that. A Catholic priest came down and we prayed. I got back to my cabin at around 9:00 p.m. Around 3:30 a.m. that morning I got up to sit out on our balcony. As I sat there alone, listening to the waves lapping against the side of the boat, feeling their gentle lull, I wept. Looking up into the cloud covered sky, I asked the Lord to give me a sign that He was with me. I needed a reassurance of his presence before I could lie down and find rest. So much was rushing through my mind. All of Delight's past, all of her struggles, it had all ended. No more than a minute later, a beautiful shooting star blazed across the sky that had been covered by clouds a moment ago. I felt His presence wash over me. In the midst of my grief, the beauty of the bond of love in marriage illuminated the night. I had no idea that I was capable of accessing depths of love like that. Once she was gone, I found out how much I really had loved Delight, and it was an incredible discovery. It was way beyond any struggles we'd ever had, or any of the darkness we'd faced. My love is so strong because God is Love. The purity of that knowledge enveloped me like a warm blanket.

I knew the Father had answered me. I went inside to lay down again for a while before I started packing up our things. I was stunned and in shock. Yet, I was in love with being in God's presence and the knowledge that there is no limit to the depths of His love. Being married made us one in flesh. And, when Delight was pulled from me and not here anymore, the clarity of that love came shining through. There on that boat, I found the most amazing, magnificent love I had ever experienced.

As I prepared to leave, in the back of my mind, I was bothered by the fact that the doctor hadn't shown up to give me any final words regarding Delight. It made me feel odd, like there was something wrong. I wondered if the doctor had made some kind of mistake with her. Why had this simple procedure that we'd done in the hospitals before gone so terribly wrong this time?

It's hard to function after the death of a loved one, but my mind was clear, so that helped. A young woman from the ship helped me with all the details and organizing that needed to be done. She had someone from the nearest island, St. Martin, meet me and help me get Delight to the funeral home. The priest that I had spoken with the night of her death came to say goodbye. The Lord was keeping me strong.

I got her to a funeral home and got checked into a hotel. I hadn't been eating or drinking, nor had I slept much. I still wasn't sure if the doctors might've done something wrong. I knew that they couldn't do an autopsy on the island. Someone from the U.S. would have to fly to the island to do the autopsy. But then I thought, what purpose would it serve to find out if they *did* do something wrong?

Wondering if perhaps the doctors had overdosed her, I called my buddy Craig for advice. Craig spoke with a friend who was a lawyer. The lawyer's advice was that I should follow up on my feelings because I wouldn't have a second chance if I didn't do it then. So I prayed about it and thought about it. In her will she said she hadn't wanted an autopsy. If the Lord hadn't wanted her to go, she wouldn't have gone. Through the years of struggle her body just couldn't take it any longer. I didn't want to drag anything out. I wanted to keep the ending beautiful and simple.

Even if there had been a mistake, there was no use sullying Delight's death with a lengthy legal battle.

It took me a day or so to pray about it and put it behind me. As I accepted the signs the Lord gave, I realized that He had been preparing me for Delight's departure. He was with me. He was very present. Her battle with Satan had been tremendous, and she never broke free from it. I knew she was with our heavenly Father and now free from Satan's attacks. I accepted that this would be a new chapter in my life. The Lord blessed me with the time I got to spend with her. We accomplished a tremendous amount together. She helped me be a man of God and fully understand what marriage was about. Delight and I both had our fair share of pain and battles with Satan, but in those dark times and struggles, we both found redemption. Delight was freed by death to be with her Redeemer, while I tarry here, on a new mission to spread the liberation, light and love or our Lord Jesus Christ.

I arrived on the island Wednesday, but couldn't get a plane out until Monday. It was a long stretch of time to be alone after what had happened, but I knew I wasn't truly alone. While I was on St. Martin, I would walk to the beach. During one of my walks, I heard James Taylor's song, "You've Got a Friend," drifting on the air from the boardwalk. I sat down at a little table nearby and just let the tears wash down my face. The song reassured me that my Jesus was with me. It was a deep moment as I rested in his love and companionship. My sisters, Pam and Penny, along with some dear friends from church were getting ready to come down and be with me, but I told them it would be okay. I could stay by myself and experience what I was going through. I walked down the boardwalk and wandered into a shop that sold different wood carvings. I found a beautiful 4 foot by 4 foot statue of Jesus and decided to buy it so I would never forget this amazing, life-changing experience. I started talking with the shop owners, and I told them what was going on in my life at the moment, and they sold me the statue for half price. It was a large and cumbersome carving and would pose a lot of trouble getting it to the States, but I never wanted to forget that through the pain, I'd discovered the depths of God's love. That statue would memorialize my experience here. Today, it rests in the foyer of my new home reminding me of the deepness of the love my Heavenly Father showed me.

I moved at the pace of the island. It was too beautiful to be in a hurry, so I slowed down, trying to relax. I started eating again. It was difficult however, as the chair across from me was empty, reminding me of Delight. I couldn't stop tears from forming and falling down my face. Now, I know that even though it seemed I was alone, Christ was sitting in that chair across from me.

My last couple of days on the island I spent getting to know a few of the locals. Saturday I went on a cruise to the Dutch side of the island. I ended up taking the same ferry as the cab driver who'd driven me there. As we boarded the ferry together, we began to talk. I went with him to visit some of his friends, but I got a little overwhelmed and just wanted to be alone. That night I started talking with another cab driver, Nate the Great. He took me to dinner and told me he was reading *A Purpose Driven Life*, by Rick Warren, so I asked him if I could go to church with him on Sunday.

On Sunday morning I found myself in a little Methodist church with about ten other people, including my new cab driving friend. After introducing me to his pastor, he shared that he'd been so touched by my story the night before, that he had written a song. It so happened that the guy who was supposed to come do music at the church didn't come, so they asked him to perform the song that he'd written. As I sat there in that humble church, listening to my friend's song, a fresh wave of the Lord's presence washed over me.

Later, I gave my new friend all of Delight's clothes to give out at the church, and when I got back home, I planned on packing up the rest of her clothes to give to them. I'd also decided to send them a monetary donation as well, to help their church as much as I could.

By now I was at peace with the Lord about Delight's death. The island had helped me find that by providing the space and quiet I'd needed to experience the depths of the Lord's love. During the five days I was there, I asked Him for guidance on how to best say good-bye to her and how to plan her memorial service and funeral. Finally, I made it back to Miami, then to Baltimore-Washington International Airport, and then, home. I knew God's manifest presence would be at her funeral service, I had no doubt. Delight's funeral was held at our church, Church of the Redeemer, and I held tight to the Lord's love. There were many who'd come to pay their last respects, and the only way I could manage to give a testimony about her was by His grace and by resting in the knowledge that she was now free. It was comforting to listen to our friends and family give testimonies about Delight. A friend called our marriage a "partnership of equals." I was the "man with the hands," and she was the "woman with the brains." Another friend and old business partner spoke of Delight's tenacity and hard-working nature. Another talked about how freely she gave her love. One of my sisters, Penny, said that Delight was bigger than her body—her body couldn't contain her essence. And in the end, that was the truth.

I rest assured in the peace that Delight is now home with her Savior, who unblinkingly embraces us in the face of the messiness of our lives. Isaiah 57:1 says, "...the righteous are taken away to be spared from evil" (NIV). Her pain and suffering has ended, and she has true and lasting peace and freedom from everything that sought to bind her on this earth. She tried to fight her demons, but in the end, no one could force her to let go.

It's so important that you finish the healing process God has laid out for you. You have to be willing to let go. You have to make that choice for yourself. Christ has promised you life, and He has promised you life abundantly. It can be frightening to let go of your past, your hurts, your addictions, your shame, especially when it's all you've ever known. But, God has so much more to give you. He wants you to live in the light, and not in the darkness. He will pour out His love upon you. Just as the father welcomed the prodigal son home, your Heavenly Father awaits you with open arms. He is welcoming you home.

Chapter 15

A New Mission

After Delight's death, as I stepped off the plane that had brought me home, I knew I was stepping into a new life for myself. God's overwhelming love that had carried me in the islands continued to surround me. I went through the motions of my normal routine at home, but a question hung over my head, dogged my heels, and skirted the edge of my consciousness. *What does God have planned for me now?*

Initially that question was easy to answer. I quickly threw myself into creating and accomplishing a to-do list. Busyness is a great distraction for avoiding, or at least postponing, uncomfortable questions. And there was much to keep me busy—planning Delight's funeral, cleaning out her clothes, moving out of our large house into a smaller cottage on our property, and work. It took about two months to clean out our old house. Once I was settled into the cottage, I felt as if I was getting more and more ready to start my new future.

My friends rallied around me, encouraged and comforted me. For them too, they wondered, "Now what?" Many of these conversations turned to questions of remarriage. I knew I wanted to remarry; after all there was that prophecy about having a baby. Carmen and her husband Terrance had also given me a word from the Lord. God told them He was going to move Delight out of my life so that I could have a wife who would partner with me in ministry. They had received this word before Delight had passed, but did not share it with me until after her funeral. I wasn't even sure if it was appropriate for me to be thinking about remarrying so soon after Delight's death. Many of my well-meaning friends cautioned me to take it easy, grieve fully, and allow myself to heal. But taking things slow had never been my style.

As I pondered my next moves, I asked the Lord to lead and guide my steps. I knew He heard me. Now, I just needed to hear Him. I was on the lookout for His signs. Thankfully for me they weren't long in coming.

One Sunday shortly after returning home, I went to church and discovered that Bishop Jackson was beginning a series on how to find a godly mate for marriage. The timing couldn't have been more perfect. The Lord knew I needed some guidance and here it was in a four part sermon series! The Bishop encouraged me to read *Boundaries in Dating* by Drs. John Townsend and Henry Cloud. Despite my reluctance to read, I pored through the book, looking for insight and direction. I was committed to doing this the Lord's way, which meant not my way. So I gave the Lord my "list" of what I hoped for in a wife... and waited.

I also knew that I needed extra counsel and advice before making any major decisions so I went to see Dr. White, my long time mentor and friend. He had been one of the teachers who had taken me in over the summer when my parents were divorcing. He was a skilled counselor with a specialty in grief counseling. Since he was also a Christian, I knew he would be able to give me godly advice and wisdom. I asked him what he thought about me seeking a new wife and desiring to have a child at my age. He had nothing but encouragement for me. He reassured me that my desires weren't out of bounds and that I should continue to chase my dreams and embrace this new life ahead of me.

However, I wasn't done yet with seeking advice on my new journey. I met with my friends Craig and Mary Kay. They knew my heart and my past better than anyone, especially Mary Kay. I told them that I was ready for a new journey, and that I didn't need to dwell on the past but wanted to move ahead into the new future God had promised me in St. Martin. Once again, I received encouragement to pursue my dreams and follow the Lord's guidance.

During this time I went on a few dates with women who were young and attractive, but were not believers. I didn't feel right about going out with them, but I did anyway. Obviously, doing it the Lord's way hadn't fully penetrated my heart. I knew right away that I was out of balance and not working with the Lord. My friend Carmen kept telling me that I needed a "like spirit" to be with. She'd say, "Joe, if she isn't a Christian, you have no business going out with her!" Then I heard a radio sermon about Samson and how his pursuit of ungodly women cost him his calling to be a leader of God's people. That brought me up short. If there was one thing I knew, it was that I wanted to be used by the Lord to minister to men and women who had been incarcerated. I decided I wasn't going to let anything come between God and His call on my life. I continued to look, but focused on women who had a heart for the Lord.

There was one lady I had my eye on that I knew was a godly woman. Maria was also a leader in Celebrate Recovery at Church of the Redeemer. She had led a variety of women's groups over the previous seven years including co-dependency for women and a domestic abuse group. She was a gifted teacher, compassionate, and dedicated to her women. Everything about her was attractive to me.

The Celebrate Recovery leaders met on the first Saturday of the month for training and team building. I usually missed those meetings, because I was serving in the jail. I decided to attend the upcoming meeting in hopes of having an opportunity to talk with Maria. I had no idea how I would manage to steal a few minutes with her, but I knew my heavenly Father could set it up if He wanted to. As I pulled into the church parking lot, wondering if this was the right thing to do, I heard another sermon begin on the radio. The topic? Samson. God was making it clear He wanted me to pursue only godly women. With this "coincidence" I had another sign. I was encouraged and emboldened to continue pursuing Maria.

The meeting began as normal, with the twenty-five or more leaders in a large group discussing concerns or questions. Then our director, Craig, asked everyone to break up into their ministry teams to meet. I happened to be in the same team as Maria, along with four or five other people. Interestingly however, no one else from the ministry team was at the meeting that Saturday. I had thirty minutes of uninterrupted time to talk with Maria!

About a week later, I worked up the nerve to email Maria and invite her to a concert and to dinner. Much to my surprise, she turned me down! Instead, she suggested we meet for coffee at church the following weekend. That meeting was the first of many, in which we began to form a friendship and get to know each other. Since we were both in recovery, we already knew quite a bit about each other. Our conversations quickly deepened as we shared about our past hurts, present victories, and hopes for our futures. Both of us knew that the Lord had to be the center of our relationship. We prayed together often and shared about what He was doing in our lives. After just a few weeks of dating, I knew I was in love with Maria. She, however, needed a bit more convincing.

I had planned a two week trip to Georgia and Florida to meet with several friends and family members. Before leaving on the trip, Maria and I had dinner together. As we said our good-byes in the parking lot, she leaned over to give me a hug, and much to my surprise, a quick peck on the cheek, before getting in her car and driving away. After that small sign of affection, I was on cloud nine! That was all the encouragement I needed to leave on my trip confident that I was making headway.

I spent a lot of that trip praying about my relationship with Maria. Was it going to work out? Was this the Lord leading us together? Would Maria return my love? As I was driving down the interstate on my way to Orlando, pondering these questions, and asking the Lord for a sign or some guidance, a truck drove past me. On the back of the truck were the words, "Consider it done." I had my sign. The Lord was telling me to relax and allow Him to work. He was in control. And so I returned to Maryland, confident that the Lord would work out any issues in His own way and that He would be working in Maria's heart to draw us together.

Maria has her own story of how the Lord was at work in her life during this time. She was leading a women's study for Celebrate Recovery that involved dealing with many hurts from the past. The Lord used this study to gently guide her into healing the hurts from her past marriage, as well as from her childhood. Her cry to the Lord was, "teach me what it means to be loved." And He responded by showing her greater depths of His own love. As her heart was healed from the past, it was opened to receiving new love from her heavenly Father, and from me. That freedom allowed her to love me in return.

◆————————————————————————◆

Maria's Story

I stared at the email in front of me—dumbfounded. I ran downstairs to my roommate and said in a shocked voice, "I think Joe Tarasuk just asked me out!"

"What?!"

"Yeah, he just asked me to go to a concert with him! This is not OK. This is definitely not OK. He's only been widowed a few months!"

I felt a mixture of feelings—shock, curiosity, and even flattery. I knew Joe and respected his walk with the Lord and his passion for helping the incarcerated. I was not opposed to getting to know him better, so since we were working on a project together for Celebrate Recovery, I slyly emailed a counteroffer.

"Joe- I'm afraid I'm not available to attend the concert, but how about meeting up for tea/coffee after church at the café to talk about the prison pen pal exchange?"

Over the next several weeks Joe and I continued to spend time together. He shared his vision for setting up a recovery center, his quest for understanding and guidance in his walk with the Lord, and his desire for a family. All of that by our third date. This man was not wasting time!

Just as Joe shared with me about his life, I also shared with him about mine. I came from a large Italian family, with two older brothers and two younger sisters, along with nine nieces and nephews. I had been a middle and high school social studies teacher before becoming a curriculum writer and eventually supervisor of social studies instruction in my school district. I was proud of my accomplishments including a Masters degree in Education.

I married my first husband when I was twenty-five years old. My husband, however, soon relapsed into alcoholism and abusive behavior towards me. Seven years later, I was so desperate to end the pain in my life I was contemplating suicide. A counselor directed me to a Celebrate Recovery group at a local church. Through the support of the women in my sharing group, I eventually gained the strength to leave my husband and not return.

After finally breaking free from that abusive relationship, the steps and support I found in Celebrate Recovery helped me turn to the Lord again to rebuild my life. Things were chaotic a roller coaster of emotions for several months, but gradually things began to settle down. I learned to listen to myself and trust my feelings. I learned to find out what I enjoyed doing, and do those things. I learned to have friendships with other women that were healthy and supportive. I learned to forgive my former husband and I learned to forgive myself.

After two years of attending Celebrate Recovery, I was invited to become a leader and facilitate the sharing group I had been a part of previously. Over the next few years I helped lead groups for domestic abuse and violence, co-dependency, and teenage girls. I began to teach in the large group meetings of 150-200 people a few times each year. I supported many women as they entered Celebrate Recovery and needed the support of someone who had been in the valley too.

When Joe and I started seeing each other, I was in the middle of leading a group of about twenty women through a study of the Celebrate Recovery steps and pointing them to trust in Christ, as they found deep healing for many of their wounds. It was incredibly fulfilling and amazing to see God do what he does best! As a leader of this group, I was also a participant, completing the same questions and books in the study. I had decided that my recovery focus during this process would be my father. I knew this would be a key for enabling me to receive and experience love and intimacy. I believe it was part of God's plan for me to work through these issues prior to marrying Joe.

As Joe and I continued to see each other, it was soon clear that Joe had made up his mind about me, but it took me a bit longer. After all, I was pretty happy with my life as it was! I had been divorced for five years, owned my own townhouse, had a good job, and had plenty of friends and hobbies. Not to mention, I hadn't been in a serious relationship with anyone in quite a while, and my last choice of a husband hadn't turned out so well. I had vowed to never make that mistake again and let another man control my life. I was going to be very careful moving forward.

I knew that I was at a crossroads. Joe was offering me a life that would center around the ministry of recovery. It would no longer be just what I did in my spare time, like a hobby. It would be central to my life, for the rest of my life. My other option was to stay single, keep ministry as part of my life, but it would be more on the sidelines. As I pondered these things I kept asking the Lord, "Is this from you?" It seemed as if the Lord had brought Joe and me together, but still I hesitated. What if I married Joe and then realized that I really missed my single life? What if I no longer was able to get outdoors and enjoy my own passions? What if I lost myself, my identity again in another person? What if Joe's vision took over my life, and I didn't like it? What about a vision for my life?

With all these questions in my mind, I sought the Lord hard. I prayed, I listened, I read his Word, I prayed more. He reminded me that he was a good father, who gave good gifts to his children. So if I believed Joe was a gift from God, then I could be assured that his gift was good. As I let this soak into my heart more and more, I felt my defensive fears start to melt away. It wasn't long before I was able to tell Joe that I was "in" for the adventure of a life time.

◆——————————————————————————◆

This was new territory for me. Maria's love and acceptance was something I had never experienced. Delight and I had loved each other, but our pasts had kept us from knowing how to express it or how to receive it. I had learned from my marriage class how important it was to serve your mate, to do more than just go through the motions, while being obedient to God in both my heart and in my actions. I had learned that it is often the little things that can make a marriage come alive. During the past two years with Delight, I had worked hard to serve her as Christ would have served her. My friend Michael called me every week to ask, "Are you treating her like Christ would treat her?" He kept me accountable to staying obedient, even when things were very difficult.

I prayed that as Maria and I grew closer, I would stay obedient to the Lord, serving her as Christ would. As my affections were received openly, without judgment, from

Maria, I felt a freedom and peace I had never known before. When you're in a relationship without baggage of the past weighing you down, the joy and peace is amazing. I know God had given me a precious gift in Maria. That summer I asked her parents' permission for me to marry their daughter. I wanted to do everything right this time, honoring both her and her parents. They gave me their blessing and welcomed me into the family. And, it was a big family! With four brothers and sisters, and nine nieces and nephews, my "family" had suddenly tripled in size! The love and acceptance I felt from them was beautiful. They were so happy for Maria and eager to get to know me and include me in the family gatherings.

The rest of 2009 was a whirlwind of activity. I was finishing the construction of a house, a remodel of the original house I grew up in. When I began the remodeling years earlier, I never guessed that it would be a new home for a new wife. God's timing is amazing. Maria and I were dating when it was time to choose many of the appliances, fixtures, colors, and designs for the house. Maria was able to put her own personality into the construction. The dry wall was finished at the end of November, and we had five weeks to complete construction to be able to move in. Only God could take a five year project and bring it to completion within days of our wedding.

We were married on January 2, 2010. The ceremony was joyous, a true celebration of God, His faithfulness, and His power to redeem even the most broken of lives. We were blessed to be surrounded by so many of our friends, many who had come through deep struggles themselves and who understood the power of God's grace in our lives.

Our life together begins!

Bishop Jackson married us and Craig and Mary Kay prayed over us and our new life together. I cried through much of the ceremony. I was so touched by the beauty of the moment and all it meant to me.

As I look back to the last few years of my life, it was obvious that the Lord had been preparing me for a new journey. Just as David was prepared as a shepherd for his future life as a warrior and king, God had been preparing me as well. This was clear to me while attending a men's retreat just before getting married. We watched the movie, *Facing the Giants*, and saw how the Lord was able to bless those who had prepared and were ready for him when the time came. During my twenty-one day fast prior to leaving on the cruise, He had clearly told me to do several things: get a grip on my finances, create time in my schedule to pursue a new mission, and be ready when the mission came.

I had been steadily getting my finances in order since the fall of 2008. I had left much of that part of the business in the hands of Delight and the other office workers. The finances were complicated and I preferred to just let others deal with them. God knew this wasn't an attitude that He wanted in His son, so He began working on that in me. Gradually, I began to shed off some debt and pick up the financial reins of my company. In 2009, we had the most prosperous year we had ever had in the twenty year history of the company. I used the gain to pay down some business debt and lay a strong foundation for the future. I also committed to opening up some of my work time to finish writing and promoting this book. I also knew I needed to take time for ministry opportunities the Lord would bring to me.

Throughout our honeymoon, Maria and I talked and prayed about where the Lord was leading us. My heart had always been led to build a residential recovery center for men and women struggling with many of the hurts that we had both been through. My vision was that this would be a place, where they could deepen their relationship with Christ and examine their past hurts, habits and hang-up in order to be free from those mistakes. My vision didn't stop there, however. I knew that these men and women would need more support than just one year of participating in a recovery program.

So part of my vision includes "Hope Homes." These will be homes, sponsored by local churches, to house our graduates as they build new lives staying connected to a community of faith. My dream was more than a hope. I was taking steps of faith to make it happen. I drew up Articles of Incorporation for "CrossRoads Freedom Center" and began to work on achieving our non-profit status. My dream was a big one, but I knew God had placed a desire to help hurting people in my heart. It was a calling I couldn't walk away from.

Before we could begin pursing our dreams, however, the Lord knew we needed a nudge. A nudge out of the ministry nest we had been nurtured in for so long. Since both Maria and I were now attending Bishop Jackson's church, we could no longer serve in the Celebrate Recovery ministry at Church of the Redeemer. Like most churches, Redeemer has a church policy requiring all ministry workers to attend the church. Although it had been difficult at the time to stop serving in that ministry, it seemed as if the Lord had "cleared the decks" to enable us to branch out in new directions. This was a huge step of faith for us. We both loved serving in Celebrate Recovery. It had been a significant part of our lives, both spiritually and even socially. But the Lord had clearly guided us to be under the teaching of Bishop Jackson, and we had to listen to the Lord.

That fall, I went on a men's retreat with my church. I was really hoping to hear from the Lord and get some direction. On Saturday morning, a young man came up to me that I had just met. I had spoken to him briefly the day before, mentioning my dream of one day opening a center.

He said he had been thinking about me all night and that the Lord had awoken him to give him a word for me. The young man told me, "You will be an architect of a center. God has a detailed plan for how this will work out, so don't worry. It will be like Moses building the tabernacle. Follow my directions closely. It's going to happen soon." Amazed at this prophecy, I knew I had my word from the Lord!

The day after I got home from the retreat, my friend Craig gave me a call. He and his wife Debbie were real estate agents and were very excited about a property they wanted to show me. "It would be a perfect recovery center," he said. The property was a former restaurant on sixteen acres. It had a twenty-five room building, three cottages, and a full restaurant kitchen on it. It had been built in 1862 and was used as a sanitarium for women for many years, and then, a restaurant for the previous thirty years. The property was in foreclosure and had a price tag of about $525,000. It was an amazing price considering it had been on the market a year earlier for $1.5 million.

It was approaching December, 2010 when this new opportunity arose. I knew I needed the Lord's guidance. Rather than do my typical five to seven day fast before Christmas, I decided to do a twenty-one day fast instead; I had a lot to pray about. Maria and I were coming up on our one year anniversary. We were trying to start a family. Craftmasters was slowing down and we needed more work. And most importantly, this new property was available. I knew the Lord watched as I fast, and I knew I would hear from Him.

It was clear that if we bought the property, the buildings would need a lot of work. The place has been in a state of disrepair for years with the previous owners doing just what was necessary to keep their restaurant open. As we inspected the place we made our lists of necessary repair—floors, drywall, insulation, windows, heater, new wiring, heat, and lots of paint. Thankfully a new roof had been installed recently, as well as a newly paved parking lot and driveway. The property also came with three large garden plots the restaurant had used to grow all of their own vegetables.

As we learned more about the property, we also discovered that it was famous for being one of the most haunted buildings in Maryland. The restaurant had frequently hosted "ghost tours" and welcomed groups of paranormal experts who used special audio and video equipment to capture evidence of spiritual activity. Witches visited the property, séances were held in some of the rooms, and drug activity was frequent among the current tenants. My experience with the spiritual realm had taught me not to take the spiritual powers lightly. If we hoped to use this site for God's glory, it would need some serious spiritual cleansing to retake the property for His kingdom.

Finally, after two months of prayer, fasting, counsel, inspections, and financing arrangements, Maria and I became the official owners of the property that would become the future home of CrossRoads Freedom Center. The dream was no longer a dream, it was a reality. As excited as I was to see this day finally come true, it was also daunting. We had a lot to do.

During 2011 a faithful crew of volunteers renovated the kitchen and the downstairs dining rooms. We rewired the electricity, installed a fire alarm system, refinished floors, replaced windows, and painted, painted, painted! What had once been a creepy, haunted house was now a bright and cheery space. We rebuilt a beautiful slate sidewalk and entranceway, cleaned up the flower beds, and trimmed many of the overgrown shrubs and trees. Most importantly though, the first year was also a time of clarifying the vision of CrossRoads. As we grappled with how to use the property, we were drawn back to the central vision to open a group home for men and women to find freedom from their bondages. Anything other than that was a distraction.

By the end of our first year, I knew we needed fresh guidance from the Holy Spirit. We had gotten a lot done, but so much more was needed. In particular, I needed help with managing our progress and guiding the vision. Everyone was looking to me for direction, but I needed leadership help if we were going to move beyond just renovations. I decided to do a forty day fast. I wanted to be like Jesus, so if he did a forty day fast, then so would I. During my fast, the Holy Spirit spoke to me in several ways. The first was clarifying my vision for CrossRoads. Like a magnet, the vision would draw people to us, but only if it was clear and in line with the Lord's original call to me. I learned how important it is to remember and re-acknowledge the Holy Spirit in this work. As I see the Holy Spirit working in, through, and around me, my faith grows. He continually makes the *logos* (written scripture) of the Bible become *rhema* (alive scripture) to me.

It was only a few months later that the Lord began to answer my prayer for help in leading my vision. I met three men, John, Mark, and Dennis, who would become soldiers by my side. The three of them had taken part in Chuck Colson's Centurion program. The program equipped men and women to become leaders to transform their communities. They had spent the previous nine months praying about what the Lord wanted them to do. Recovery, re-entry, and working with veterans was on the top of their list. I met them at a prayer meeting and they asked me to share about CrossRoads. They immediately knew that this was no coincidence and that God had meant for us to meet.

It wasn't long before John, Mark, and Dennis were regulars at CrossRoads, getting to know Maria and me as well as the other volunteers. The four of us began meeting each week to discuss updates and next steps on the property. John took over many of the organizational aspects like paying bills, setting up an accounting system, and creating a web page. These were things that Maria and

I couldn't keep up with since we were both working full time. More than anything I benefited from their counsel and insights. They helped to give me direction and focus. It seemed that 2012 was going to be a year of building relationships that would be a foundation for CrossRoads. Although our volunteers had been meeting every Saturday to work on the property, we decided to be more intentional about building our relationships with one another. Our Saturdays now began with at least 30 minutes of worship and prayer, followed by a hot breakfast and finally the work for the day. Then about noon we'd break for lunch. Two friends came each weekend to prepare the meals, hosting from fifteen to twenty-five volunteers each weekend. As the word began to spread among our friends and in the community, of what was going on at CrossRoads, more and more people showed up at our door offering to help however they could. In some cases the people showing up were looking for something else. Parents concerned about the addictions of their own children came seeking counsel, encouragement and hope. It was heart-breaking to see the pain that addiction was causing these families. It only served to fuel our motivation to be a place of refuge and hope for the hurting.

That summer we had our first fundraising event. We called it a "Friendraiser" with the goal of letting our family and friends hear about what we were doing and see our progress. We hosted a BBQ, set up tents and outdoor games, worshipped together, and shared a video that included my testimony and the vision for CrossRoads. We were blown away when over 250 people attended the event!

CrossRoads is becoming a place where people feel the presence of God. As one of our Board members said, "I can't leave here without knowing I've had an encounter with God." There have been many miracles that have occurred, most what some would consider "small"- like when I prayed for an electrician to come help us and one showed up 30 minutes later! Or when we needed landscaping fabric for the garden, and we found some hidden in the brush-cut to the exact length and width needed. Our biggest miracle however happened in December. At the time we had two men living on the property. In exchange for a place to live, they kept an eye on the property and helped with maintenance. Dan was one of these men. He shared with us the devastating news that he had been re-diagnosed with cancer. This time it showed up in his lungs in several places. After an overnight in the hospital for tests, he was sent home until his next appointment when the doctors and he would decide on the treatment that would most prolong his life. That Saturday, Maria, Mark and Robin, another volunteer, prayed for Dan. They asked God to replace his lungs with new lungs and restore him to full health. Two days later Dan returned to the hospital. After running scans on his lungs, the doctors found no traces of cancer! Our prayer is that CrossRoads will continue to be a place where God's power and presence become more and more evident. What a start we've had already!

2012 was a year of great victories and progress, but it has not been without a lot of effort. Maria and I made many financial sacrifices to keep the property going- paying the electric, refilling propane and oil tanks, buying food for the weekend events. We sold one of our cars, a Mercedes, for a Hyundai, we sold jewelry and pieces of gold I had, every extra cent we had went into CrossRoads. We had some help along the way of course, but after two years we had put in over $250,000. Sometimes we wondered if God would provide the resources we needed, but somehow we made it. By the end of 2012 we were astonished to find out we had raised over $50,000 in donations from just a few fundraiser events. This was a huge confirmation that the Lord was with us.

As 2013 is beginning, Maria and I are continuing to do all we can to bring our vision to life. Our house is on the market to be rented or sold so we can move onto the property in Ijamsville. We'll be trading an 8,000 square foot house for a 1,000 square foot cottage. But we couldn't be more excited!

CrossRoads will require the support of many people and churches, but I'm in it for the long haul. Families, men, and women need help breaking the cycles of addiction, depression, and bad choices that have kept generations from living in freedom. We can't wait for the government to help people. It's up to the Church, the body of Christ, to take the gospel of freedom to them. If we let our pride and differences keep us from fulfilling God's call to help the less fortunate, we all suffer. Our communities, schools, businesses, prisons, shelters, churches—they are all impacted. But we can make a difference. We can help change the world--one center, one church, one home, one person at a time.

It took me twenty-five years to get to this point from when the Lord first saved me. I've been on the streets. I've been incarcerated and brought to Christ. I've sustained a successful business, and also become a builder of houses. I've served in church, in Celebrate Recovery, and now this. Christ brought me into contact with people like Reverend Talbert, Chuck Colson, Rick Warren, John Baker, Bill Smith, Pastor Dale O'Shields, and Bishop Harry Jackson. All have played a role in the journey.

This journey with God has been a journey of faith, compassion, and love. I've learned that it is possible to have an intimate relationship with a beautiful and multi-faceted Lord. He is my Father, my God Almighty, the one who blesses, nurtures, sanctifies, provides and leads me. He has brought me through some dark places. Because He did, I have discovered the many wonderful ways He expresses Himself and seeks to know His children.

This book is part of the vision for CrossRoads Freedom Center as well. The fact that you are even holding it in your hands is evidence of God's ability to accomplish the impossible. All money received from the sales of this book will go into the CR Freedom Center to build our group home, gym and worship center, as well as to remodel the Inn, so that it can be used to support our recovery ministry. If you were inspired by this book, we invite you to follow our progress on Facebook and at our website: crfreedomcenter.com. You can also make a direct donation from our website if you are led to support this work. And if you live in the area, come join us at 8a.m., Saturday mornings to lend a hand!

I believe we can help change the world. When the Church follows Christ, it is the most powerful force on earth. If you have been touched or moved by my story and the work ahead for CRFC, please remember us in your prayers. Without the prayers of the righteous, we will never be victorious. All things are possible. I hope you'll join us in the mission. If an uneducated street dealer can get this far, what about you?

CrossRoads Freedom Center

CrossRoads Freedom Center Site Map

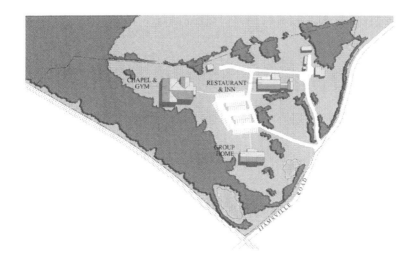

Chapel and Gymnasium

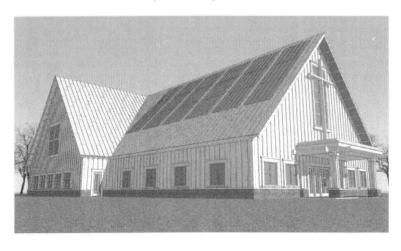

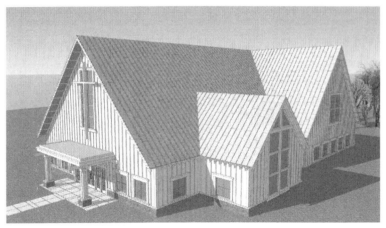